JN281779

幕末・明治の工芸

世界を魅了した日本の技と美

Japanese Crafts of the Late Edo and Meiji Periods

Masterpieces of Skill and Beauty

世界を魅了した日本の技と美

幕末・明治の工芸

村田理如（清水三年坂美術館館長）

淡交社

Contents

Kyoto Cloisonné of Namikawa Yasuyuki 18
Owari Cloisonné and Works by Namikawa Sosuke 34
Kyoto Satsuma Ware 56
Inro 68
Netsuke 80
Sword Fittings 88
Metalwork 102
Lacquer 118

English Text 143
List of Objects 159

幕末・明治の工芸　目次

幕末・明治の工芸、その技と美に魅せられて　村田理如 6

清水三年坂美術館のコレクション　ヴィクター・ハリス 8

【作品図版】

並河靖之の京七宝 18

尾張七宝、そして涛川惣助 34

京薩摩 56

印籠 68

根付 80

刀装具 88

金工 102

蒔絵 118

評価される細密工芸　原田一敏 136

英文テキスト 143

収録作品一覧 159

幕末・明治の工芸、
その技と美に魅せられて

村田理如（清水三年坂美術館館長）

The Beauty of Late Edo and Meiji-period Crafts
Masayuki Murata

　その時、私の目はショーケースの中の2つの印籠にクギ付けになっていた。この世にこれほど繊細で凝縮された美の世界が存在するなんて…。今から20年前のニューヨークはマンハッタンでの出来事である。それがきっかけで、以来私はコレクターの道を歩むことになる。

　幕末・明治の工芸品、それは多くの日本人にとって未知な存在といっても過言ではない。その名品の多くは海外に存在し、日本人の目にはほとんど触れることがないからである。今でも日本の市場に名品が出れば、すぐに海外の業者の手に渡り、海外のコレクターや美術館に収まることになる。

　幕末・明治の工芸品が海外で人気があるのは、まず文句なしに美しいからである。そして作品の持つ品格と高度な技に圧倒されるからである。それは金工にしろ蒔絵にしろ、武家社会をパトロンとして発展し、明治においては、帝室技芸員制度や皇室の支援があったこととも関連している。

　江戸時代、将軍家や大名家にはお抱えの金工師、蒔絵師たちがおり、刀装金具や印籠、嫁入り道具などの調度品を作っていた。大きな戦もなく、平和な時代が長く続き、鐔などの刀装金具は、やがて高度な装飾技法を駆使した美術品へと姿を変えていく。印籠なども、携帯用の薬入れから、細密な蒔絵をほどこした装身具へと変化した。

　そして明治維新。武家社会が終焉を迎え、金工師や蒔絵師の失業者が巷に大量にあふれ、彼らの多くは輸出用の商品の制作に携わることになる。しかしその一方で、名工たちは皇室や上流階級の需要を満たすため、刀装金

具や調度品作りで培った高度な技法を使って花瓶や香炉、煙草箱、硯箱、香箱等の制作に力を注いだ。彼らの作品は当時、世界各地で開催された万国博覧会にも出品され、非常に高い評価を得ることになる。

やがて日本国内に急速に欧米の文化が流入し、日本人のライフスタイルも変化し、美術の分野でも欧米に追随するようになる。日本人の多くは日本の伝統工芸よりも欧米の文化に興味を持ち、名工たちの作品も、時を置かずして日本人の脳裏から忘れ去られることになる。

こうして内外で高い評価を得た幕末・明治の名品は、今も海外に流出し続けているのである。

世界に誇れる工芸の最高峰、幕末・明治の工芸品が今でも海外で高い評価を受けているのに、本家本元の日本人が評価もしないし、何も知らない。こうした現状を日本の方々に知ってもらい、幕末・明治の工芸品が日本でも正しく評価されること、そして多くの美術館に誇らしく飾られることを願って、本書を出した次第である。

また本書の執筆にあたっては、多くの書物をはじめとする先賢の研究を参考にさせていただいた。そのいちいちは記さないが謝意を表したい。

清水三年坂美術館
のコレクション

ヴィクター・ハリス（大英博物館・アジア部名誉日本部長）

The Collection of the Kiyomizu Sannenzaka Museum
Victor Harris

　清水三年坂美術館の収蔵品は、1868年の明治維新以降の数十年間にヨーロッパとアメリカに輸出された、江戸時代（1600-1868）と明治時代（1868-1912）の特上の工芸品の数々である。この時期の日本は西欧の文物を急速に採り入れるのと並行して、江戸時代の生活様式のある部分を排除する。たとえば1876年に施行された廃刀令は士族の帯刀を禁じたため、萌芽期にあった古美術品の輸出市場に無用となった刀が洪水のように流入することとなった。西洋式の服の着用がひろまるにつれ、装身具のなかにも廃れるものが現れる。印や常備薬を入れ、ひもを通して帯に付ける印籠、そのひもを帯に挟む飾りも兼ねた留め具の根付などである。伝達手段の変化、とりわけ印刷術の導入により伝統的な木版刷りは旗色が悪くなった。ペンとインクが徐々に筆と硯、そして古来の蒔絵の硯箱の出番を奪ってゆく。こうして刀剣と金工の刀装具、印籠、根付、精巧な蒔絵の硯箱が初めて西洋の蒐集家にも手の届くものとなった。

　江戸時代は全期を通じて日本が近隣諸国との間に平和を保っていたのに対して、ヨーロッパ諸国はほぼ休む間もなく互いに争い、あるいはインド、アジア、アフリカの各地に帝国主義的な領土拡張戦争をしかけた。したがって、さまざまな文化の産んだ刀剣をふくめて、厖大な量の武器が自由に流通する状況にあった。どこの国のものと比べても、日本の刀剣が武器としても、芸術品としても抜きんでていることは、だれの眼にも明らかだった。日本の刀剣は機能面から他国の産に優るばかりでなく、蒔絵をほどこした鞘、柄に添える小道具（拵え）の装

飾性の高さも、たちまち西洋の愛好家の注目するところとなった。

　日本の漆芸品は、オランダの東インド会社が長崎から輸出した箪笥、棚などの家具を通じて、17世紀以来ヨーロッパでも知られていた。磁器がヨーロッパでは「チャイナ」の名で知られたように、漆芸品は「ジャパン」と呼び習わされることになる。ヨーロッパでも漆芸品を模倣しようとする試みが行われて、たとえば「セラック」などが開発されたけれども、日本で制作された本物の品質に比肩することはできなかった。江戸時代に輸出された漆芸品は総体として良品ではあったけれども、当時の武士、貴族、豪商らの求めに応じて制作された硯箱、香箱、小箪笥の比ではない。1859年に横浜が開港して間もなく徳川幕府が漆芸品の輸出を容易にする政策を採ったのも事実ながら、明治維新以前にはこれらに匹敵するものはヨーロッパに紹介されることがなかった。

　イギリスの外交官ラザフォード・オルコックは1862年の第2回万国博覧会に、おもに日用品からなる日本の産品の大がかりな収集品を展示した。しかし1867年のパリ万博に14歳の徳川昭武を代表とする一行が持参した百点あまりの品々は、それに比べてさらに質が高い。この時展示されたのは江戸時代に日常的に用いられた武器、武具、陶器、華麗な染織品、漆芸品などである。

　明治時代の初期には、伝統工芸が日本にとって他国の産業に太刀打ちできる分野であり、連続して開催された万国博覧会で日本の工芸品は高い評価を受けた。1873年にウィーン、1876年にフィラデルフィア、1883年にアムス

テルダム、1885年にはアントワープ、1888年にバルセロナ、1893年にシカゴ、1900年にパリ、そして1904年にはセントルイスで万博が開催された。

　明治時代の職人たちは、当然ながら輸出向けの装飾品の制作に手を染めた。海外の蒐集家は熱心にこれらを買い求めた。たとえばロンドンのヴィクトリア・アンド・アルバート美術館は1852年にロンドンのヒューイット商会から「長崎」の漆芸コレクションを買い入れたのを皮切りに、1876年のフィラデルフィア万博に展示された多くの陶器をはじめとして、さまざまな万博で、また多くの業者から多数の品々を購入する。パリ万博に展示された鈴木長吉の巨大な香炉には、1500ポンドもの高額を支払った。ヴィクトリア・アンド・アルバート美術館は「優美な形態を按配し、調和のとれた色彩を組み合わせ、デザインの原則を実用に供した品々を生産者、職人、一般大衆のために展示する」ことを目的に開設された。この分野こそ、日本の匠の独擅場といってよい。伝統的なデザインは新鮮で刺激的であり、西欧の反応を参考に古来の意匠に新味も加えたデザインを、日本の職人が伝統的な技能を用いて制作した輸出用の品々も見事なできばえだった。

　美術館も熱心に蒐集したけれども、明治時代の最良の品々は、富裕で目利きの蒐集家の手に落ちた。これらの品々は輸出向けに制作されたため、天皇と宮内省が購入した少数を除いて、日本国内にはほとんど残らなかった。今日では国立近代美術館などの専門的な美術館と、東京国立博物館などの大規模な博物館にそれぞれ少数が収

蔵されているにすぎない。ところが19世紀後半から20世紀前半にかけて制作された工芸品の重要性に対する認識が深まるにつれ、海外に出かけて少数ながら失われた自国の文化遺産をとりもどそうとする蒐集家が日本にも現れた。清水三年坂美術館の館長を務める村田氏は、長い年月をかけて現在世界で入手可能な高品質の品々の最も重要なコレクションを築きあげた。刀装具の伝統的金工と輸出向けの品、漆芸品、「薩摩」型の装飾的な彩色陶器、明治期の最上の工人の手になる優れた七宝がその内容である。

　後藤一乗、加納夏雄など江戸末期から明治にかけての名匠の手になる刀装具は、同美術館がヨーロッパやアメリカから買い戻した装飾的な小道具が揃うことで本来の姿となった。加納夏雄が芍薬を彫り、象嵌した銀製の懐中時計の外ケース（図版172）は、西洋の工芸品と日本的装飾の対照がきわだつ独特の味わいを備える。応永期（1394-1428）の刀工源左衛門信国の鍛えた脇差には、正阿弥勝義の「蝶紋金総金具堆黒鞘合口拵え」が揃っている（図版125-127）。この拵えは正阿弥勝義の名品と呼んでさしつかえない。この拵えは大名かそれに匹敵する高位の武士の委嘱により制作されたもので、おそらく日本を離れたことはないと思われる。廃刀令の後に勝義が手がけた、色金の高浮彫りで雄鶏と雌鶏をかたどり、これを象嵌した装飾性の高い銀の香炉（図版166-167）とは好対照をなす。

　伝統的な日本の金工の魅力の一端は、西洋にはそれまで知られていなかった合金の彩りの豊かさと製造技法

に求められる。鏨の角度と深さを変えて、紙に筆で描いた墨の線を模す技法は片切彫と呼ばれ、これによって匠は絵を描くように金属に図柄を彫りつけた。優雅に錆ついた鉄の古色、赤銅の名で呼ばれる銅に少量の金の入った黒ずんだ合金、四分一の茶色味や銀灰色の美しさ、また金、銀をはじめとする多様な彩りの金属の象嵌によって、装飾美術に新たな可能性が拓けた。

　そうした金工は当然ながら非常に高価ではあったが、当時の西欧社会には富の配分に大きな格差があり、富裕層は芸術、工芸を尊重した。当時の人々は万国博覧会に展示された品々を、ちょうど今日の私たちがオリンピックで選手の活躍を見て覚えるのと同様の感動をもって迎えたのであり、日本は万博で入賞し続けたのだった。

　最高峰の漆芸品はヨーロッパのセラック、中国の漆、江戸期の輸出品と比較され、それらをはるかに凌駕するものと高く評価された。金工と同じように、漆芸は高級美術の手段であり、絵画と彫刻を異国風に、そして斬新にとりあわせた技法であった。漆に金粉をほどこした金蒔絵は、あたかも純金のような外観が好まれ、とりわけ人気を博した。ヨーロッパ人は、建物が金で覆われた「ジパング」について記したマルコ・ポーロのことばを思い出したにちがいない。このほかにも少量の金を用いて輝きを添える日本ならではの技法もいくつかあった。西洋には相当するもののない梨子地は金などの粉末の上に半透明の漆を塗り、澄んだ夜空に輝く星のような効果をあげる。西洋では明治時代になって初めて紹介された江戸期の印籠には、蒔絵のあらゆる技法が用いられており、

江戸末期の金工職人と同じように、漆芸家も万博の展示用に通常よりも大きな作品を制作した。

　宝石などの貴重品を収める古来の手箱などのような実用品もあれば、白山松哉が太陽の下に鷺を、月の下に烏を描いた素晴らしい蒔絵額のように純粋な装飾品もある（図版197-198）。この一対の蒔絵額は漆芸の技巧の冴え、一度見れば忘れがたい構図の美しさ、そして優れて「日本的」な主題など、一級の芸術品に求められるすべての要素を備えている。日本に限らず、これほど充実した、質の高い作品は現在世界中どこでも制作されていない。印籠には洗練を極めた根付がつきものである。ミニチュア彫刻と呼ぶにふさわしい根付は、明治初期に江戸文化の生き生きとした姿を諸外国に伝えた。今日、私たちが根付を見れば江戸時代に帰ったような気分に浸るのと同様である。清水三年坂美術館は、制作当時のままに根付の揃った状態のよい印籠のえり抜きの品々を収蔵している。

　開明的だった明治天皇は日本の芸術、工芸が世界ではたすべき役割を充分に理解した。天皇は日本同様、ヨーロッパとアメリカ合衆国でもよく知られると同時に敬愛され、また皇室は日本文化を国際社会に紹介する労をとり功績を挙げた。天皇は個人としても国内の展示会で作品を買い上げて工匠を支援した。1890年に催された第3回内国勧業博覧会で最も高価な品物を買い上げたのは、皇室と少数の外国人蒐集家だった。それに先立ち京都で開催された日本美術協会の展覧会で天皇は32点、皇太后は18点、宮内省は27点の作品を購入している。天皇は

次回の博覧会のために、2万円もの巨額の寄付をおこなった。さらに宮内省は海外の賓客や王室のために、皇室を表わす菊の御紋入りの贈り物の制作を委嘱した。贈り物に選ばれたのは対の銀の花瓶、七宝の花瓶、蒔絵の箱物などである。刀剣が委嘱された例もあり、英国初代大使クロード・マクドナルド卿には菅原包則作の太刀一振りが贈られた。この刀は現在ロンドンのヴィクトリア・アンド・アルバート美術館に収蔵されている。以来約4世代の交替に要する時が流れ、一族が零落すれば家宝がやむなく市場に出ることもある。清水三年坂美術館はそうした歴史的名品の数々を入手し、かつてはヨーロッパの堂々たる邸のドレッサー（飾り棚）を飾ったであろう傑作が、初めて日本の愛好家の目に触れることになったのである。

　清水三年坂美術館はこのほかにも、京都をはじめ各地の窯元で制作された釉をかけ、薩摩の産地にその名をちなむ陶器、そして日本独特の七宝細工の優れた作品を多く収蔵する。薩摩藩の藩主は1867年のパリ万国博に使節を派遣し、金を多用した彩色陶器（白薩摩金襴手）が大いに好評を博した。薩摩藩のさらなる成功を受けて、陶器のこうした形状、装飾法をとりあげる陶工が京都の錦光山、藪明山を先頭に、各地に現れる。薩摩風の装飾が最大の効果をあげるのは、金をふんだんに用い、鮮やかな色彩で綿密に描いた華麗な小品においてだろう。その質の高さは西欧の陶工にはまったく想像のつかないものだった。とはいえ、西欧人の目に何より強い印象を残したのは、おそらく七宝細工ではなかろうか。金属をエナメルで被う技法の伝統はヨーロッパにも古くからあり、

フランスのシャンルヴェには優れた工匠がいた。中国の七宝も広く知られるが、こちらは日本の七宝の繊細さと瑞々しさにおよばない。いずれも帝室技芸員に任じられた涛川惣助、並河靖之の作品など、最良の七宝に見る針金細工の繊細さと色彩の瑞々しさは、西洋の芸術家の能力をはるかに上まわる。清水三年坂美術館は、今後もけっして色褪せることのない日本工芸の黄金時代の代表作を保有するといっても過言ではないだろう。

（翻訳／木下哲夫）

・本書に収録した作品はすべて清水三年坂美術館の所蔵品です。
・本書の各項解説文（pp.18-135、文＝村田理如）は、京都新聞「海を渡った工芸美術－幕末・明治（2004年7月－2005年4月連載）」を一部加筆修正して収録いたしました。
・収録の作品名称、作銘の読みは、原則的に通例にしたがいました。また印籠・根付作品については、銘を記載、その他は、作者名あるいは工房名を記載しました。
・英文テキストは、本書所収の日本語文を翻訳し、巻末にまとめたもので、一部、英文読者のための加筆あるいは省略をおこなっています。なおpp.8-15のハリス氏の日本語原稿は和文翻訳したもので、原文は英文テキスト頁に収録いたしました。

作品図版

PLATES

解説＝村田理如
清水三年坂美術館館長

Masayuki Murata
Director, Kiyomizu Sannenzaka Museum

並河靖之の京七宝

Kyoto Cloisonné of Namikawa Yasuyuki

　私が並河靖之（1845-1927）の作品と初めて出会ったのは、今から十数年前のロンドンのギャラリーでだった。手にとって間近で見たその時の感動は生涯忘れることはない。
　美しい金線や銀線で複雑に装飾された枠の中に、赤や緑や青の色が黒を背景に鮮やかに浮かび上がり、花や鳥などの文様が幻想的な雰囲気をたたえていた。しかも今から百年以上も前に作られたと知ってさらに驚いたのである。器体は今作られたばかりのように美しく、意匠もまったく古さがなくあか抜けていた。
　多くの人はおそらく、その時の私同様に並河靖之の名をご存知ないだろう。しかし、私が館長をしている清水三年坂美術館（京都市東山区）で並河靖之たち明治の七宝作家の作品を目にした来館者は「明治の日本にこんなに美しい芸術品があったのだ」と感激される。
　日本の七宝の歴史は奈良時代以前にさかのぼる。しかし盛んになったのは幕末以後。それまでは、いくつかの七宝技術が門外不出の技として釘隠しや刀の鐔の装飾などに細々と使われていた。
　近代の七宝は、名古屋の梶常吉（1808-83）が幕末に、オランダ人商人から購入した七宝細工（おそらく中国製）を分解して有線七宝の技術を解明、作品に取り入れたことに始まる。京都にも明治初めに伝わり、並河靖之は「有線七宝こそ日本の七宝の本流」と考えて、七宝を工芸品から芸術品に昇華させていった。
　有線七宝の製作の大筋は以下の過程を経る。まず銅で作られた胎（器などの素材）に下絵を描き、絵にそって平べったい金線、銀線、真鍮線などを蘭から採ったノリで貼り付ける。さらに銀ろうを付けて窯で1度焼き、線を固定する。次に、線で囲んだ枠の中に七宝粉を筆で入れ、窯で焼いて七宝を胎に付着させる工程を6、7回繰り返し、線が完全に隠れると砥石で表面を研ぐ。

[1] 桜蝶図平皿
Plate with butterflies
and cherry blossoms
径24.6cm

目の粗い石から細かい石まで6、7種類砥石を換えて何度も研ぐ。かくも多くの手間と人件費を要したことが、伝統工芸のなかでもいち早く衰えたことの一因になったのだろう。

並河靖之は川越藩近江領の代官・高岡家の三男として京都に生まれた。11歳の時、縁者の並河家当主が急死、その養子に入った。並河家は青蓮院宮家に仕えたが、副業として七宝細工を始めていた。靖之は宮家に仕える傍ら、明治6(1873)年に七宝の製作を始め、明治8年の京都博覧会に作品を出した。

作品の繊細さ、優美さ、品格、色彩感覚、画面の構成力が海外で非常に高い評価を受けた。明治9(1876)年のフィラデルフィア万国博覧会、明治11(1878)年のパリ万国博覧会などで受賞、明治22(1889)年のパリ万国博覧会では金賞牌に輝いた。国内でも明治10年の第1回内国勧業博覧会、明治23年の第3回内国勧業博覧会で受賞した。国内外での受賞は31回(金賞11回、銀賞7回、銅賞4回など)におよぶ。

作品はほとんどが海外の富豪や美術館に買い取られ、高さ10センチほどの小さなものですら、そのころロンドンで働くセクレタリー(事務職)の給与1年分に匹敵したとされる。日本人には手の届く価格でなかった。

明治29(1896)年に帝室技芸員に任命され、宮内省(現、宮内庁)に納めた作品は海外の要人に贈られた。作品は自らの工房を除くと日本にはほとんど残らず、たまに日本で見つかる作品も明治天皇からの御下賜品が大半だ。

並河靖之の作品はまれに30センチを超えるものもあるが、多くは高さ5センチから20センチ程度の小ささ。世の中には、ほどほどに小さいが故に美しいといったものが存在する。たとえば宝石、根付、ミニアチュール(細密画)、パウル・クレーの絵。大きくすると間延びして、しっくりとこない。同じことが並河靖之の作品についてもいえそうな気がする。

[2] 蝶図瓢形花瓶
Gourd-shaped vase with butterflies
高さ18.0cm

[3] 花蝶文花瓶
Vase with design of flowers and butterflies
高さ16.0cm

[4] 藤図花瓶
Vase with wisteria
高さ25.0cm

[5] 春秋遊技図扁壺　一対
Pair of drum vases depicting spring and autumn pastimes
高さ15.0cm

[6] 裏面

［7］花鳥図花瓶
Vase with birds and flowers
高さ16.5cm

［8］蝶草花文飾り壺
Jar with design of flowers and butterflies
高さ8.8cm

［9］花蝶文飾り壺
Jar with design of flowers and butterflies
高さ11.7cm

[10] 花文飾り壺
Jar with floral design
高さ12.0cm

[11] 蝶図香合
Incense container with butterflies
径6.0cm

[12] 花鳥図棗
Tea container with birds and flowers
高さ6.7cm

[13] 花蝶文香水瓶
Perfume bottles with design of butterflies and flowers
高さ7.0cm

並河靖之は、黒色釉薬を発明したことで知られるが、その他によく用いられる靖之独自の色として、ここに見られるようにモスグリーン、アイボリー、ライトグレー、あずき色などがあげられる。靖之の作品の特色の一つとして同じデザインで色違いのものを作ることがあげられる。これは他の作家にはまったく見られないことである。色に対するこだわりが人一倍強かったことがうかがわれる。

また靖之の作品には蝶がモチーフとしてよく使われる。並河家の家紋が蝶であることと関係しているのかもしれない。

[14] 花文飾り壺
Jars with floral design
高さ9.0cm

並河靖之の京七宝

［15］花鳥図飾り壺
Jar with birds and flowers
高さ8.8cm

この作品も靖之の形に対するこだわりが強く感じられる。靖之独特のモスグリーンの釉薬にピンクやグリーンの草花が美しく映えたこの作品は、特に使用目的があって作られたものではない。丸味をおびた偏平な本体に可愛らしい蓋が付けられており、独特の美しいフォルムを形成している。

[16] 芦カワセミ図飾り壺
Jar with kingfisher and reeds
高さ15.0cm

[17] 紅葉鳥図飾り壺
Jar with birds and autumn foliage
高さ18.5cm

最晩年に作られた靖之独特の薄茶色のボディーに金線で山水風景を描いた作品。蓋や本体の覆輪は銀でなく、銅と金の合金である赤銅を用いている。これも晩年作の特徴の一つである。また金線の太さを自在に変え、金線を釉薬と同じように色彩の一つとして使用している(右)。
イギリス人ハーバード・G・ポンティングが出版した日本紹介の書籍に並河工房の紹介とともに掲載されている作品。説明書には、明治天皇からの注文で作られている、と書かれている(下)。

［18］山水図香炉
Incense burner with landscape
高さ11.0cm

［19］葵祭図花瓶　一対
Pair of vases with festival scene
高さ23.5cm

尾張七宝、そして涛川惣助
おわりしっぽう　　　なみかわそうすけ

Owari Cloisonné and Works by Namikawa Sosuke

尾張七宝
Owari Cloisonné

　幕末に尾張（愛知県）で生まれた有線七宝は、技術的に未完成のまま明治を迎える。他の工芸品、陶磁器や蒔絵、金工などが長い歴史と伝統を持っていたのに対し、有線七宝は生まれたばかりの技術であった。

　当初は中国の七宝に近く、いわゆる泥七宝と呼ばれる不透明な釉薬を使っていた。また植線の間隔が広すぎると焼成時にヒビが入るため、多くの無駄な線を入れる必要があった。そうしたことから絵画的表現には限界があった。

　ところがその後、有線七宝は蒔絵や金工が何百年もかかって進化してきたことを考えると、信じられないようなスピードで進化を遂げることに成功する。その進化に大きく貢献した一人のドイツ人科学者がいた。ゴットフリート・ワグネルである。ワグネルは慶応4（1868）年に来日し、有田（佐賀県）をはじめ日本各地の陶工たちに世界最先端の成型技術や焼成技術を指導した。

　また、名古屋や京都では陶磁器だけでなく七宝の釉薬の改良にも取り組んだ。日本の七宝技術は飛躍的に改善され、ムダな植線を入れなくても、胎（地金）に広範囲に釉を焼き付けることが可能になった。鮮やかな色彩の透明釉も作れるようになった。そして日本の有線七宝は、明治10（1877）年を過ぎるころから輸出工芸品の大きな柱に成長していったのである。

　当時の七宝生産の中心地は、海東郡遠島村（現、愛知県海部郡七宝町）だった。遠島村を代表する七宝作家に林小伝治（1831-1915）がいる。小伝治は、有線七宝の発明者、梶常吉の直弟子・林庄五郎から七宝の製法を学び、文久3（1863）年には開業して

[20] 四季草花図花瓶
林小伝治作
Vase with flowers of the four seasons
HAYASHI Kodenji
高さ23.5cm

いる。海外貿易にもいち早く取り組み、品質の高い作品を生み出した。釉薬の開発や改良にも積極的に取り組み、遠島村に陳列館を建設、七宝補習学校も設立し、近代七宝の発展に大きく寄与した。当時、七宝の植線には一般に真鍮線が使われたが、小伝治の作品の多くは金線、銀線を用い、高級感のあるのが特徴であった。小伝治の他に今でも海外で人気の高い尾張七宝作家に、粂野締太郎（1863-1939）、川出柴太郎（1856-？）、服部唯三郎、安藤重兵衛がいる。

粂野締太郎は植線の細密さで知られ、とても人間わざとは思えない驚異的な作品を残している。川出柴太郎は、今に続く安藤七宝店の工場長としても活躍した名工で、作品数は非常に少ないが一作一作異なった題材で丁寧に作った。また服部唯三郎や安藤重兵衛は川出とともに技術面で常に七宝界をリードした。部分的に釉を植線面より盛り上げて付着焼成する盛上七宝や金属胎に彫金をほどこし、その上から透明釉を焼き付ける透明七宝の技法は、彼らが最初に使ったといわれている。

また当時、日本の七宝は技術的にも世界の最先端を走っていたが、一つだけフランスに追い越された技術があった。それはプリカジュール（省胎七宝）と呼ばれ、胎を硝酸で溶かして植線と釉薬部分だけを残す技法だった。これも川出柴太郎と安藤重兵衛がすぐに日本で再現した。

このように日本の七宝界はおもに尾張の人たちが技術的にはリードしてきたといえる。一方、これらの新しい技法は、京七宝ではほとんど使われることはなかった。京都は並河靖之を中心として従来の有線七宝を進化させることで発展していった。尾張と京の七宝はそれぞれの道を歩んだのである。

[21] 花鳩図花瓶
林小伝治作
Vase with doves and flowers
HAYASHI Kodenji
高さ50.0cm

尾張七宝、そして涛川惣助 | 37

[22] 蝶図花瓶
林小伝治作
Vase with butterflies
HAYASHI Kodenji
高さ35.0cm

京七宝の作品には靖之の発明した黒色釉がよく使われているが、尾張七宝の作品には黒色釉が用いられることはほとんどなく、昔ながらのナス紺と呼ばれるナスビの紺色に近いダークブルーの背景が使われている。
林小伝治は、並河靖之や涛川惣助と同じく高級品の市場に的を絞って、細密作品を手掛けたことで知られる。なかでも金線や銀線を用いて作られた蝶をモチーフにした作品は、靖之の作品とはちがったリアルさが特徴で、その植線技術は驚嘆に値する。

[23] 鳥図香合
林小伝治作
Incense container with birds
HAYASHI Kodenji
高さ7.7cm

[24] 蝶図小箱
林小伝治作
Small box with butterflies
HAYASHI Kodenji
縦10.0cm　横12.0cm　高さ4.0cm

［25］藤図飾り壺
　　　林小伝治作
Jar with wisteria
HAYASHI Kodenji
高さ12.0cm

［26］側面

［27］花鳥図花瓶
林小伝治作
Vase with birds and flowers
HAYASHI Kodenji
高さ30.0cm

尾張七宝、そして涛川惣助

[28] 群蝶文小箱
粂野締太郎作
Small box with pattern of flocking butterflies
KUMENO Teitaro
縦7.0cm　横9.0cm　高さ3.7cm

[29] 部分拡大

粂野締太郎の群蝶の作品はいくつか知られているが、その植線の細密さと根気には脱帽させられる。この小箱には数千匹の蝶々が植線されているが、いったいどれだけの日数をかけて作られたのであろうか。銀線を植線したあと、そこに釉薬を入れて窯で焼く作業を5〜6回繰り返すが、この細かい枠に釉薬を入れていく作業も想像を絶する。

[30] 粟鶉図鉢
川出柴太郎作
Squared flower-petal bowl
with quail and millet
KAWADE Shibataro
高さ20.0cm

[31] 側面と内側

[32] 深山雉図花瓶
　　　伊藤銘
Vase with pheasants and mountain scene
Signed "ITO"
高さ45.0cm

[33] 牡丹図花瓶
服部唯三郎作
Vase with peonies
HATTORI Tadasaburo
高さ16.0cm

[34] 龍鳳凰文花瓶
　　安藤重兵衛作
Vase with dragon and phoenix design
ANDO Jubei
高さ45.0cm

[35] 紅葉草花図花瓶
無銘
Vase with autumn foliage and flowers
No signature
高さ30.0cm

安藤は自社でも七宝を製造していたが、林小伝治をはじめ七宝町の多くの窯元からも仕入れ、自社銘を入れて販売していた。そのため、作風で安藤製を特定するのは難しい。

[36] 鷹図花瓶
　　　無銘
Vase with hawk
No signature
高さ45.0cm

[37] 牡丹図花瓶
無銘
Vase with peonies
No signature
高さ40.0cm

涛川惣助
Works by Namikawa Sosuke

　さて、明治の七宝の歴史のなかで忘れてはならない巨人がもう一人いる。赤坂離宮（現、迎賓館）の「花鳥の間」（大食堂ならびに小食堂）を飾る32枚の額を製作した東京の涛川惣助(1847-1910)である。涛川惣助は下総国鶴巻村蛇園（現、千葉県旭市）に生まれ、明治12（1879）年には無線七宝を完成させている。無線七宝の技法は、途中までは有線七宝と同じだが、最終的に線を全部取りはずしてからもう一度窯で焼き付ける方法で、線の一部だけをはずしてから焼く省線七宝もある。この技法は、線を除いた部分だけ色の境界がぼやけるため、日本画的な表現が可能になる。

　惣助は最初、陶磁器の貿易を仕事としていたが、明治10（1877）年の第1回内国勧業博覧会で七宝作品を目の当たりにし、七宝の魅力にとりつかれ、ただちに七宝製作に取り組んだとされる。同年、ドイツのアーレンス商会が亀戸に持っていた七宝工場を手に入れ、そこで働いていた尾張の七宝工たちを指導して、明治12年には無線七宝を完成させたといわれる。また明治20（1887）年には名古屋の大日本七宝製造会社の東京分工場も手に入れた。こうした経緯からみると惣助の七宝は、尾張七宝との結びつきが強いともいえる。

　彼は日本画を七宝で表現することを目指した。しかしその作品は単なる日本画の写し替えではなく、七宝でなければ表現しえない奥行きのある質感を持った作品に仕上がっている。

　涛川惣助はこの功績によって、京都の有線七宝作家、並河靖之とともに明治29（1896）年、帝室技芸員に選ばれた。帝室技芸員の歴史のなかで七宝ジャンルから選ばれたのはこの二人だけであった。

　惣助は生涯、無線七宝、省線七宝の技法で日本画的な表現の作品にこだわり続けた。一方、京都の並河靖之は、他の作家たちが惣助の影響を受けて無線・省線の技法を取り入れるなかで、最後まで有線七宝で通した。金線や銀線こそが七宝の美しさを生み出す重要な要素だと考えていたのだ。まことに対照的な二人であった。

[38] 舟鷺図皿
濤川惣助作
Decorative plate with boat and heron
NAMIKAWA Sosuke
横29.7cm

[39] 糸桜図皿
濤川惣助作
Decorative plate with weeping cherry
NAMIKAWA Sosuke
横30.0cm

[40] 裏面　惣助銘「魁」

尾張七宝、そして濤川惣助 | 51

[41] 藤図花瓶
涛川惣助作
Vase with wisteria
NAMIKAWA Sosuke
高さ30.5cm

［43］［44］の作品は、最終工程で植線をはずし、再度焼成することにより色の境界線がなくなり、日本画のぼかし風の表現に成功した惣助の無線七宝の代表作である。類似作品に明治26（1893）年シカゴ万博に出品され、その後、東京国立博物館に納められた＜富嶽図額＞がある。
この無線七宝発明の功績により、明治29年、有線の並河靖之とともに帝室技芸員に任ぜられた。

［42］紅白芙蓉図小箱
涛川惣助作
Small box with white and red mallow flowers
NAMIKAWA Sosuke
縦8.0cm　横9.5cm　高さ3.2cm

［43］富嶽図煙草ケース
涛川惣助作
Cigarette case with view of Mount Fuji
NAMIKAWA Sosuke
縦9.0cm　横8.0cm

［44］富嶽図小箱
涛川惣助作
Small box with view of Mount Fuji
NAMIKAWA Sosuke
縦11.3cm　横14.0cm　高さ5.0cm

［45］菊紋月芦雁図花瓶　一対
　　　涛川惣助作
Pair of vases with wild goose and reeds and chrysanthemum crests
NAMIKAWA Sosuke
高さ44.0cm

惣助は明治天皇から外国の国王、大統領、要人等にプレゼントされる菊の御紋章入りの花瓶をはじめ、宮内省（現、宮内庁）からの仕事も多く手がけた。迎賓館（旧、赤坂離宮）の食堂（バンケットルーム）の壁を飾る32枚の七宝額も惣助の手によるものである。

[46]
菊紋蛍図花瓶　一対
涛川惣助作
Pair of vases with fireflies and
chrysanthemum crests
NAMIKAWA Sosuke
高さ36.0cm

[47] 裏面

尾張七宝、そして涛川惣助 | 55

京薩摩
きょう さつ ま

Kyoto Satsuma Ware

　美術のジャンルの一つに細密美術がある。特に有名なのはペルシャ（イラン）やムガール（インド）の細密画（ミニアチュール）である。人々はより手の込んだもの、細密なものを愛するのではないだろうか。細密にすることがより美しさを増すというジャンルの話ではあるが…。
　見る側はその途方もない繊細な技術や忍耐力に驚き、作る側はだれにも真似できないほどの技を誇りに感じる。それが細密美術の世界である。
　日本においては、ペルシャやムガールのような細密画は発展しなかった。むしろ七宝や金工において細密な世界が日本独自に発展した。細密画に近いものをあげるなら、その代表格は薩摩焼であろう。
　薩摩焼は、桃山時代に薩摩や大隅（鹿児島県）の窯で朝鮮半島の陶工たちによって始められた焼きもの。苗代川窯では、幕末に金彩色絵の細緻な絵付け焼きものが作られた。
　日本が初めて参加した慶応3（1867）年のパリ万国博覧会では、単独で参加した薩摩藩が薩摩焼を出品し、高い評価を受ける。そして明治6（1873）年、ウィーン万国博覧会に「大花瓶」を出品した沈家12代・沈寿官（1835-1906）も賞賛を浴びる。この2つの万国博覧会を契機に薩摩焼の海外における評価は決定的なものとなった。その後、京都・大阪・名古屋・東京・横浜などでも薩摩風の絵付けの焼きものが流行し、その多くが輸出されることで海外における「SATSUMA」は日本陶磁の一ブランドとして定着することになる。まだ工業製品を持たなかった当時の日本にとって、「SATSUMA」は他の陶磁器や七宝と並んで日本の輸出商品の花形であった。そのなかでも京都の錦光山と大阪の藪明山は、海外での人気を二分するライバルであった。

［48］色絵金彩組輪文茶碗（部分拡大）
司山製
Tea bowl with design of concentric circles
on colors and gold
SHIZAN workshop
高さ6.0cm　径11.2cm

錦光山家は、江戸中期より続く粟田焼の名門であった。6代錦光山宗兵衛は時代の流れに敏感で、明治5（1872）年ごろには、薩摩焼の作風を取り入れた、いわゆる京薩摩の作品をすでに作り出していたといわれる。

　明治17（1884）年に父の死により家督を継いだ7代錦光山宗兵衛（1868-1927）は、父から学んだ精緻で雅やかな花鳥画を中心とした作品を製作、明治22（1889）年のパリ万博では銀賞を受賞した。宗兵衛が弱冠21歳の時のことである。当時、粟田口にあった錦光山の工房には200人を超す陶工が働き、当地随一の規模を誇っていた。

　そのころ、東山の粟田口一帯には錦光山のほかにも多くの窯が「SATSUMA」を焼いていた。「SATSUMA」には、藪明山や錦光山のほか、精巧山、版錦山、司山、明山、介山、雪山、古山など多くの銘が見られる。しかし、どれが京都でどれが他所かということはほとんど研究されておらず、錦光山風の絵付けのものを一般に京薩摩と呼んでいるようだ。

　藪明山（1853-1934）は画家藪長水の次男として大坂に生まれ、東京で陶画を学んだ。明治13（1880）年、大阪中之島に薩摩風色絵陶器の工房を築き、緻密な風景画と装飾で独自の作品を作り出し、国内外の博覧会で受賞を重ねた。一点一点手抜きをせず、密度の濃い作品を作り続けることによって海外で非常に高い評価を得ていった。

　明治26（1893）年のシカゴ万国博覧会は「SATSUMA」にとって大きな転換期であった。絶大だった人気にかげりが見えはじめた。世紀末を迎えて人々は新しいものを求め、欧州のアール・ヌーヴォーにみられるような新しい芸術運動のうねりが押し寄せていた。

　出品した錦光山の力作も低い評価しか与えられなかった。この時を境にして錦光山宗兵衛は積極的に意匠、技術の改革に取り組み、アール・ヌーヴォー調の作品を作りはじめる。一方、大阪の藪明山はかたくなに今までの作風にこだわり続け、そのなかでさらに完成度の高い作品を目指す道を選んだ。

　そして両者の作品は博覧会での評価とは裏腹に、その後も売り上げを伸ばし続けた。窯がなくなった今もなお、世界中に愛好家は多い。

[49] 色絵金彩花鳥図花瓶
7代目錦光山宗兵衛製
Vase with birds and flowers in colors and gold
KINKOZAN Sobei VII workshop
高さ40.0cm

京薩摩 | 59

[50] 色絵金彩花見図花瓶
　　7代目錦光山宗兵衛製
Vase with cherry-blossom viewing scene in colors and gold
KINKOZAN Sobei VII workshop
高さ31.5cm

　花瓶の口部分にアール・ヌーヴォー風の草花を金彩であしらった不思議な雰囲気の作品である。1900年のパリ万博で、日本の花鳥草木や昆虫をモチーフにした美術品に刺激を受けた欧州の芸術家たちのいわゆるアール・ヌーヴォーの作品が多数出品されると、それを見た日本人の陶芸家のなかにも、その様式を取り入れる人たちが現れた。錦光山もその一人であった。

[51] 色絵金彩花鳥図花瓶
7代目錦光山宗兵衛製
Vase with birds and flowers in colors and gold
KINKOZAN Sobei Ⅶ workshop
高さ33.0cm

[52] 色絵金彩花鶏図茶碗
　　　版錦山製
Tea bowl with flowers and domestic fowl
in colors and gold
HANKINZAN workshop
径10.0cm

[53] 内側

[54] 色絵金彩花蝶文鉢
　　　作者不詳
Bowl with design of birds and butterflies
in colors and gold
Artist unknown
高さ6.0cm　径11.5cm

[55] 色絵金彩洋花図鉢
7代目錦光山宗兵衛製
Bowl with Western flowers in colors and gold
KINKOZAN Sobei VII workshop
高さ11.5cm　径28.0cm

[56] 色絵金彩菊図輪花鉢
源山
Scalloped bowl with chrysanthemums
in colors and gold
GENZAN
高さ14.5cm　径30.0cm

［57］色絵金彩浦島太郎図貝合せ
　　　陽山製
Decorative clam shells with scenes
from the folk tale *Urashima Taro* in colors and gold
YOZAN workshop
高さ6.0cm　長径14.0cm

［58］内側

[59] 色絵金彩扇面文飾り壺
古山製
Jar with design of folding fans
in colors and gold
KOZAN workshop
高さ10.0cm　径10.0cm

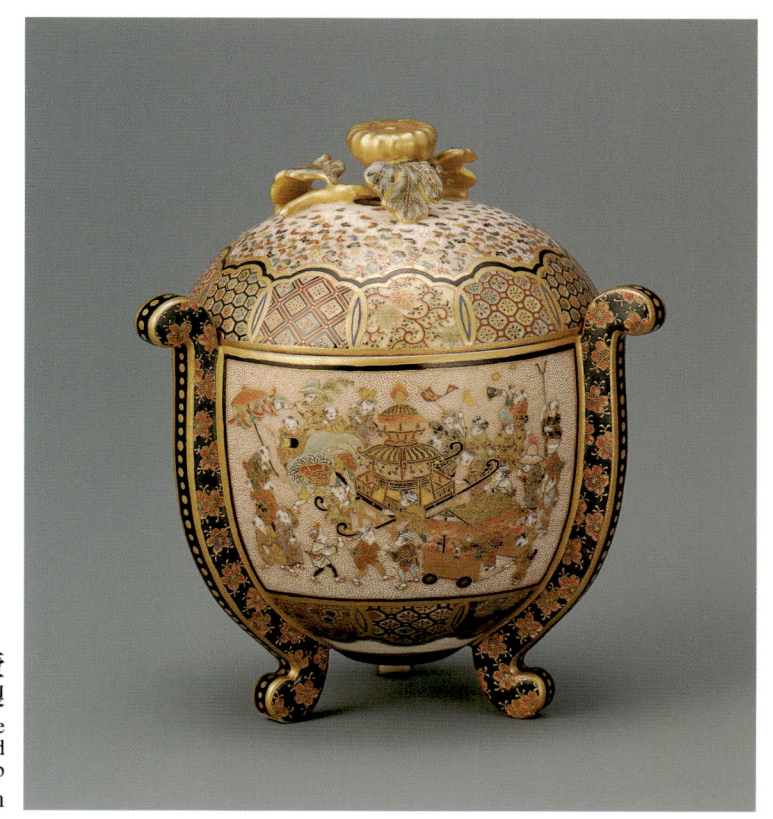

[60] 色絵金彩祭礼図飾り壺
司山製
Jar with festival scene
in colors and gold
SHIZAN workshop
高さ11.0cm　径9.0cm

[61] 色絵金彩蝶菊尽し茶碗
藪　明山製
Tea bowl with banded pattern of butterflies and chrysanthemums
YABU Meizan workshop
高さ5.0cm　径10.0cm

[62] 高台とその周辺

藪明山は大阪の窯であるが、細密で美しい作品を多く残している。高級ブランドとして欧米人の間でもてはやされた。

[63] 色絵金彩鶴花人物図花瓶　一対
　　　藪　明山製
Pair of vases with cranes, flowers, and human figures
YABU Meizan workshop
高さ31.0cm　径13.0cm

印籠
いんろう

Inro

　一般の人が印籠と聞いてまず思い浮かべるのはテレビ時代劇の『水戸黄門』であろう。悪人どもの目の前に、徳川家の家紋入りの印籠が高く掲げられると、悪人どもはいっせいに地面にひれ伏す。印籠は権威の象徴なのである。将軍家や大名家の紋章の入った印籠は古美術品の市でも時々見かけることがあるが、実際そのような威力があったかどうかは疑わしい。

　それはともかくとして、印籠は一体何に使われていたのであろうか。実は、薬を入れて持ち歩くための道具であり、旅に出るときの必需品であった。まさに水戸黄門にふさわしい小道具ではある。

　ではなぜ、薬を入れる道具が印籠と呼ばれたのだろう。印籠には、印鑑を入れるためのハコという意味もある。印籠はもともと印鑑や印肉を入れておくための道具だった。それが、江戸初期ころから薬を入れて持ち歩く道具として使われるようになったが、名称は「薬籠」とはならず「印籠」がそのまま使われ続けたらしい。印籠が薬入れとして使われるようになってから、表面に装飾がほどこされるようになる。

　印籠は将軍家や大名家だけでなく、男女を問わず旅の必需品であった。一般的には3段か4段、要するに3、4種類の常備薬を入れる小箱の集まりでできている。印籠だけが単独で使われることはなく、印籠を帯から吊すための「根付」、蓋の開閉を調節するための「緒締め」と一組になって初めて道具としての機能を発揮する。

　もっともすべての印籠が腰からぶら下げるタイプのものだったわけではなく、ふところに納めるタイプのものもあった。

　印籠本体の素材は、和紙を漆や膠で何重にも固めたものや木製のものが一般的だが、なかには金属、七宝、焼きもの、象牙な

[64] 夕立雨宿り蒔絵印籠
　　塩見政誠銘
Inro with maki-e depiction of taking shelter
from a sudden evening shower
Signed "SHIOMI Masanari"

[65] 裏面

塩見政誠は京都の蒔絵師で、研出し蒔絵の名工。この印籠も細密な絵を色絵研出しで表現した名品。研出し蒔絵は生漆で絵を描いた上に金粉や色粉を蒔きいったん黒漆で塗り固めた後、炭で表面を研ぎ、粉の中心部で研ぎ終える難度の高い技法。

どで作られたものもある。

　幕末になって、印籠の装飾性がさらに増した。単なる旅行用薬入れでなく、装身具としての比重が大きくなった。一人でいくつもの印籠を持ち、オシャレを演出する小道具として短時間の外出にも携行することが流行った。その点、現代人のネクタイと若干の共通点はあるが、はるかにオシャレで贅沢な装身具だった。

　上等の印籠には蒔絵がほどこされ、金、銀、赤銅（銅と金の合金）などの彫金された金具が象嵌されたり、象牙や鼈甲、珊瑚などの高級素材が表面の装飾に使われた。

　将軍家や大名家にはお抱えの蒔絵師がおり、主人の使う印籠は彼らが作っていたが、幕末になると大名家を上まわる財力を持った商人たちが、町の蒔絵師たちに高級印籠を作らせるようになった。依頼された蒔絵師たちも、持てる技の限りを尽くし、あるいは新しい技法を開発して魅力的な印籠を生み出していった。蒔絵や彫金の技術は江戸時代の中ごろから幕末にかけて日本の歴史上最高のレベルに達するのである。

　明治に入ると多くの欧米人が日本を訪れ、印籠の美しさの虜になる。その結果、それまでに作られた高級印籠が、大量に海外へ流出することになった。欧米には印籠の大コレクターが現れ、一人で数百本から1千本近く持つ人も大勢いた。英国の実業家トムキンソンや世界的食品会社ネスレの日本代表でスイス人のシャンプー、グリーンフィールズ、バウアー、カザール、ブッシェル…枚挙にいとまがない。こうした世界的大コレクターの集めた印籠には一級品が多く、見ごたえがある。

　残念ながら日本人で世界的に名の知られた印籠コレクターは、武井守正男爵（1842-1926）くらいで、印籠の本家本元の日本としては淋しい限りである。日本の市で一級品の印籠が出ても、すぐ海外のディーラーに買い取られる状況が続いている。

　日本人は日本の近代絵画や欧州の印象派の絵画には大金を投じるが、幕末・明治の美術品にはあまり金を出さないようだ。明治時代には、高級印籠1本で庶民の家が1軒建ったといわれる。今日では、特別高価なものを除けば、高級印籠は1本2百万円前後で手に入れることができる。印籠の大コレクターが日本にも現れることを願ってやまない。

[66] 蘭陵王蒔絵印籠
梶川文龍斎銘　金工：浜野矩随作
Inro with maki-e depiction of a Bugaku court dance
Signed "KAJIKAWA Bunryusai"
Metalwork: HAMANO Noriyuki

[67] 裏面

印籠は印籠部分が単独で存在しているわけではない。根付、緒締めと一緒になって機能を発揮する。
この有名な蘭陵王の舞手は金を高彫りして土台に接着したもので、他の部分は蒔絵や堆朱で装飾されている。根付はセイウチの牙を透彫りしたもので、緒締めは金無垢で彫ったもの。すべての面で、非の打ちどころのない最高傑作の一つである。

印籠　71

[68] 伊勢海老蒔絵印籠（シャンプーコレクション）
　　 自徳銘
Inro with maki-e depiction of lobsters
Signed "JITOKU"

スイス人のシャンプー夫妻が戦前に日本で集めた印籠コレクションは世界的に有名で、質の高さとコンディションの良さで知られていた。
総点数は500点を越え見ごたえのある作品が多くふくまれる。近年、一括して清水三年坂美術館の所蔵に帰した。

[69] 猫蝶牡丹蒔絵印籠
（シャンプーコレクション）
寿秀銘
Inro with maki-e depiction
of a cat, butterflies, and peony
Signed "TOSHIHIDE"

[70] 群盲撫象蒔絵印籠
梶川銘

Inro with maki-e depiction of the parable of the blind men examining an elephant
Signed "KAJIKAWA"

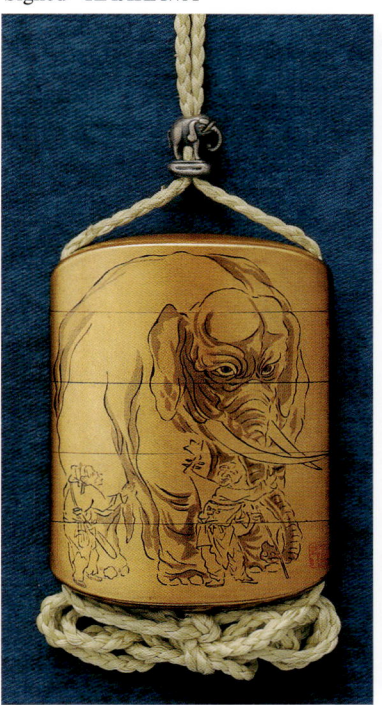

[71] 裏面

[72] 節句蒔絵印籠（シャンプーコレクション）
春照斎銘

Inro with maki-e depiction of seasonal festivals
Signed "SHUNSHOSAI"

[73] 裏面

印籠 | 73

[74] 祇園祭礼蒔絵印籠
　　　春正銘
Inro with maki-e depiction of the Gion Festival
Signed "SHUNSHO"

[75] 裏面

[76] 合戦蒔絵印籠
　　　無銘
Inro with maki-e depiction of battle scene
No signature

[77] 裏面

[78] 群鶴蒔絵印籠
　　無銘
Inro with maki-e depiction of flock of cranes
No signature

[79] 裏面

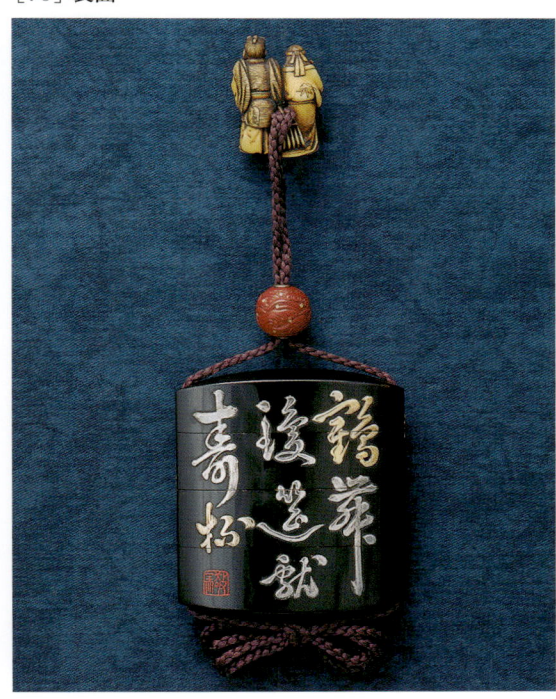

[80] 千羽鶴蒔絵印籠
　　常川銘
Inro with maki-e depiction
of thousand crane-pattern
Signed "JOSEN"

[81] 群蝶蒔絵青貝印籠
　　観松斎銘
Inro with maki-e
and mother-of-pearl depiction of butterflies
Signed "KANSHOSAI"

[82] 絵馬蒔絵印籠
幸阿弥銘

Inro with maki-e depiction of
Shinto talismans featuring horse and monkey figures
Signed "KOAMI"

[83] 裏面

[84] 吉原蒔絵印籠
松杖斎銘

Inro with maki-e depiction of
the Yoshiwara pleasure quarters
Signed "SHOJOSAI"

[85] 裏面

[86] 歌舞伎寿曽我対面蒔絵印籠
(シャンプーコレクション)
春政銘
Inro with maki-e depiction of scene from a Kabuki play
Signed "HARUMASA"

世界的には根付や緒締めだけを収集しているコレクターも多く、印籠に根付や緒締めが付いていなかったり、もともと付いていたものが別のものに入れ替わっていたりすることが多い。

[87] 傘美人蒔絵印籠
春正銘
Inro with maki-e depiction of beauties
under a parasol and a youthful dandy
Signed "SHUNSHO"

[88] 裏面

印籠 | 77

[89] 川中島合戦金工鞘印籠
　　一柳友善銘
Sheath inro with metal-inlay depiction of the Battle of Kawanakajima
Signed "ICHIRYU Tomoyoshi"

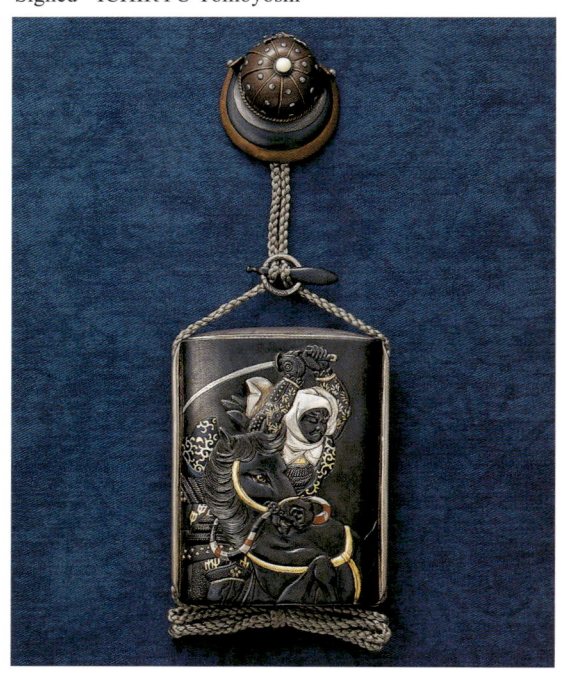

[90] 裏面

[91] 平田七宝印籠
　　無銘
Inro with Hirata cloisonné
No signature

高度な象嵌技術によって作られた珍しい金工印籠。使われている金属は金、銀、赤銅、四分一銀、素銅。緒締めを上にずらし、逆さまにすると銀製三段の印籠が出てくる鞘印籠になっている。根付、緒締めも金工で、製作時からの3点揃いのものと思われる（上）。

平田は家康の頃より将軍家お抱えの七宝師の家系。金地蒔絵に美しい象嵌七宝を配した珍しい作品（左）。

最後の将軍徳川慶喜が所有していたと伝えられる金工印籠。赤銅地に金、銀、四分一銀、素銅が象嵌された名品。鞘印籠になっており、中に銀製三段印籠が入っており、根付も緒締めも揃いの金工品で、根付の底には慶喜の慶の1字が金の本象嵌で入っている。緒締めは金無垢の鯉の高彫り。その当時、金工技術で秀でていた水戸金工の作品（右頁上）。

[92] 獅子牡丹金工印籠
　　大川元義・小泉友随合作　緒締め：義茂銘
Inro with metal inlay depiction of lion and peony
OKAWA Motoyoshi and KOIZUMI Tomoyuki
Ojime: Signed "YOSHISHIGE"

[93] 裏面

[94] 恵比寿大黒杣田印籠
　　杣田久光銘
Somada-lacquer inro depicting the gods Ebisu and Daikoku
Signed "SOMADA Hisamitsu"

[95] 菊花堆朱印籠
　　無銘
Inro with chrysanthemum pattern
in carved red lacquer (*tsuishu*)
No signature

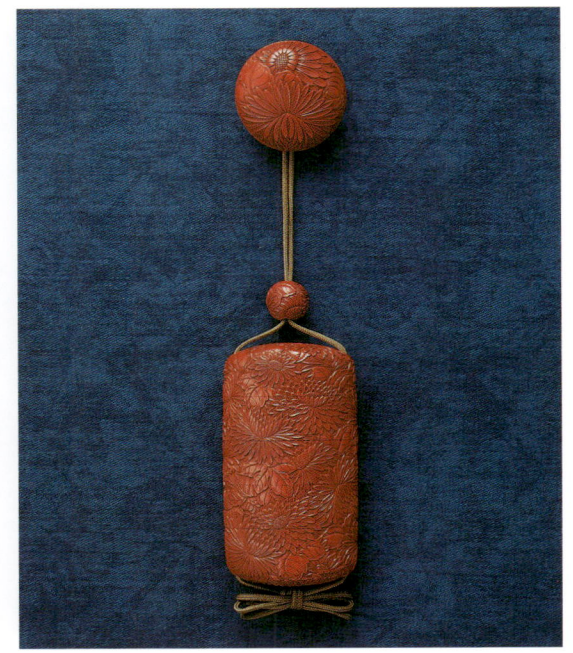

根付
ねつけ

Netsuke

　根付ほど、日本人の生活に浸透しながら私たちの目の前から急速に姿を消したものはないのではなかろうか。一昔前までは、どこの家にもあった。古い家で探せば、1、2個は出てくるはずで、私の家にも、祖父が大事にしていた根付が古銭と一緒にあった。

　根付はきものと一緒に日本人の文化の中心にあった。きものには洋服のようなポケットがない。ふところとか袂にしまいにくい重いものや嵩張るものは、腰にぶら下げた。燧袋とか巾着、煙草入れ、印籠など、提物と総称されるものがそれだ。

　最初は、提物同士をひもで結んで振り分け荷物のようにして帯の両側に下げていたようだ。しかし江戸時代初期には金属の環を帯に通して、環に提物のひもを結び付けて外出したらしい。それが江戸時代前期に、環を帯に通さず、帯の下を通して上に出す、すなわち根付形式の物入れに変化したと考えられている。

[96] 杯蝿木彫・金工根付
　　　天民銘
Netsuke of fly in a bowl, wood and metal
Signed "TENMIN"
径4.5cm

[97] 裏面

[98] 束ね薪蒔絵印籠
観松斎銘
紅葉蒔絵瓢形根付・堆朱瓢形緒締め

Inro in the shape of firewood and gourd
with maki-e decoration
Signed "KANSHOSAI"
Gourd-shaped netsuke with maki-e of fall foliage,
carved red lacquer gourd-shaped ojime

― 根付

― 緒締め

― 印籠

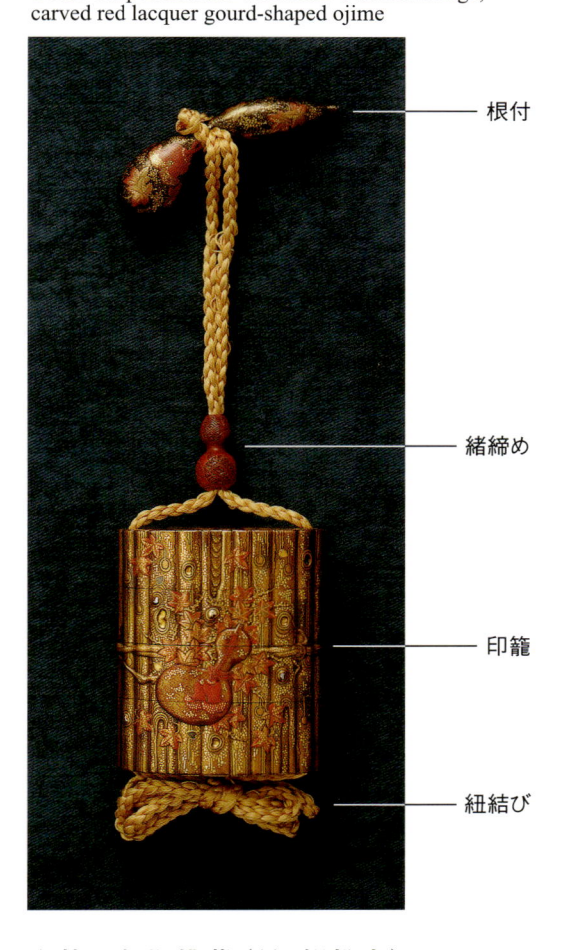

― 紐結び

印籠は飯塚桃葉（号・観松斎）の作品。薪を縄で束ねて、水筒の瓢箪をぶら下げている図である。根付も緒締めも瓢箪で揃えてある。緒締めは堆朱製。

根付にはいろいろな形状があり、形によって鏡蓋、饅頭、柳左、箱形、差、形彫根付などに分けられる。

たとえば鏡蓋根付は象牙や木製の円形台に金属板を嵌め込んでいる。饅頭根付は、扁平な円形で形が饅頭に似ているところからそう呼ばれた。柳左根付は、扁平な円形の中を空洞にして透彫りをほどこし、人物や動物などの形に彫っていて、箱形根付は蓋付きの箱形で漆塗りや蒔絵のものが多い。差根付は細長い根付で、帯に差すタイプだ。その他、動物、人物などを彫刻した形彫と呼ばれるものもある。

題材は多岐にわたり、動物、植物、昆虫、人物、神仙、架空の動物、道具類、故事伝説、仏像、能面、おばけ、妖怪などありとあらゆるものがある。

素材は木、象牙のものが多いが、動物の牙や歯、骨、爪、竹、藤、漆、金属、陶磁、木の実、硝子、石、珊瑚、海松貝など多様なものが用いられている。

根付には、機能面から種々の制約がある。きものを傷めたり、体に当たらないよう出っ張りがなく、姿のよい面が外に向くような形状と座りの良さ、ひも通しの位置などを十分考慮して作らなければならない。そういった制約のなかで作られることが、根付を魅力的で面白いものにしているようだ。

根付師たちは、自由奔放に好きな素材、好きな技法を駆使し、生き生きとした品を作り出してきた。そして、印籠が武家社会をベースに発展したのに対し、根付は初めから町人主導で発展してきた。そのためか、印籠が東京、京都を中心に作られていたのに対し、根付は岐阜とか奈良、島根のような地方でもそれぞれ特徴ある名品が生まれた。そうした根付のなかには、ユーモラスな、思わずほほえんでしまうようなものも多い。印籠にはほとんど見られない特徴だ。

根付は、印籠とほぼ同じ幕末・明治期に海外へ流出した。手ごろな小ささと高い芸術性が多くの外国人を引き付け、土産品やコレクションとして大量に海外に持ち出された。あまりにも身近な存在であったため、日本人が芸術品と気づ

かないうちに浮世絵と同じ運命をたどったのである。
　この状況にいち早く気づいたのは、郷誠之助男爵（1865-1942）であった。郷男爵は、貴族院議員、東京株式取引所理事長、東京商工会議所会頭などを歴任した大実業家で、根付の蒐集に奔走し、代表的根付師の名品を体系的に集めて、貴重な文化遺産の流出に気づかない日本人に警鐘を鳴らし続けた。郷男爵の合計272点にのぼる根付コレクションは、その死後、帝室博物館（東京国立博物館の前身）に寄贈された。
　ロンドンの大英博物館、ニューヨークのメトロポリタン美術館をはじめ、世界には1千点を超える根付を保有する博物館、美術館、コレクターは数多い。根付の研究も欧米が中心で、研究書の出版も大半は欧米からだ。郷男爵の無念は今も続いている。

[99] 秋草蒔絵鞘印籠
観松斎銘
蕨図金工根付（加納夏雄作）・珊瑚緒締め
Sheath inro with maki-e depiction of autumn grasses
Signed "KANSHOSAI"
Metalwork netsuke in fern frond design (KANO Natsuo),
coral ojime

[100] 猿回し金工鏡蓋根付
なつを銘（加納夏雄作）
Kagamibuta netsuke
with metal inlay design of a monkey
trainer and monkey
Signed "NATSUO" (KANO Natsuo)
径4.5cm

[101] 草花象牙彫饅頭根付
無銘
Ivory *manju* netsuke
with carved floral design
No signature
径4.5cm

[102] 花虫金工鏡蓋根付
無銘
Kagamibuta netsuke
with metal inlay design
of flowers and insects
No signature
径4.5cm

[103] 裏面

根付 | 83

［104］銀杏象牙彫根付
　　　光春銘

Ivory netsuke
carved in the shape of gingko nuts
Signed "KOSHUN"

幅3.5cm　高さ4.0cm

［105］蛸象牙彫根付
　　　正水

Ivory netsuke
carved in the shape of an octopus
Signed "SHOSUI"

幅3.8cm　高さ1.2cm

［106］裏面

［107］親子亀象牙彫根付
　　　無銘

Ivory netsuke
carved in the shape of parent and child turtles
No signature

幅3.5cm　高さ4.5cm

［108］裏面

[109] 蜂巣木彫・象牙彫根付
忠一銘

Wood netsuke
carved in the shape of hornet's nest
with ivory insets as larvae
Signed "TADAICHI"

幅3.5cm　高さ4.0cm

[110] 梨蜂木彫根付
江月銘

Wood netsuke
carved in the shape of wasp and pear
Signed "KOGETSU"

幅3.5cm　高さ5.0cm

[111] 裏面

[112] 蟬木彫根付
無銘

Wood netsuke
carved in the shape of cicada
No signature

長幅6.0cm　短幅2.0cm

[113] 裏面

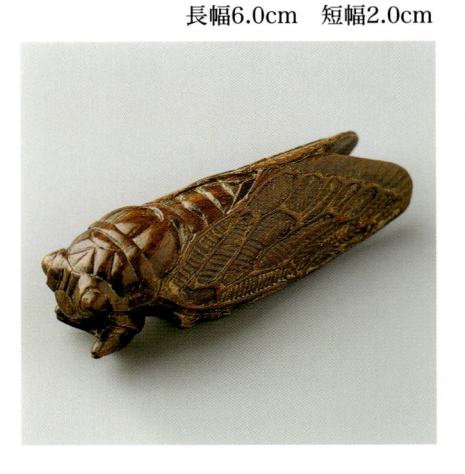

根付 | 85

[114] 落花生木彫根付
玉藻銘

Wood netsuke carved in the shape of peanuts
Signed "GYOKUSO"
幅5.0cm　高さ2.5cm

[115] 栗木彫根付
藻水銘

Wood netsuke carved in the shape of chestnut
Signed "SOSUI"
幅3.0cm　高さ2.6cm

[116] 蛇籠木彫根付
旭舟銘

Wood netsuke carved in the shape of gravel-filled basket used to reinforce river banks
Signed "KYOKUSHU"
幅3.8cm　高さ3.0cm

[117] 銭束木彫根付
旭斎銘

Wood netsuke carved in the shape of string of coins
Signed "KYUSAI"
幅5.0cm　高さ4.0cm

[118] 蛇木彫根付
無銘

Wood netsuke carved in the shape of snake
No signature
幅4.0cm　高さ2.5cm

藻派の根付は細密さと高い写実性に特徴がある。[114]の作品は殻が割れて見えている実が中で動くように作られている。[115]の栗はどう見ても本物の栗の実に見える。[116]の蛇籠の中の石は1個1個が動く。
ツゲの木の固まりを彫刻刀を使って自在に彫り上げる技術は、神技としか思えない。

[119] 越後獅子木彫根付
珉江銘
Wood netsuke carved in the shape of
Echigo-*jishi* (mythical lion)
Signed "MINKO"

幅2.5cm　高さ3.2cm

[120] 部分

[121] 獅子木彫根付
無銘
Wood netsuke carved in
the shape of *shishi* (mythical lion)
No signature

幅2.0cm　高さ4.0cm

[122] 裏面

[123] 人魚木彫根付
一雲銘
Wood netsuke
carved in the shape of mermaid
Signed "ICHIUN"

幅4.0cm　高さ2.2cm

[124] 烏天狗木彫根付
舟珉銘
Wood netsuke carved in the shape
of *tengu* goblin
Signed "SHUMIN"

幅4.0cm　高さ3.0cm

刀装具
とう そう ぐ

Sword Fittings

　海外に流出した美術品のなかで刀剣や鐔などの刀装具は比較的流出の量が少なく、流出の時期も遅かったといえる。その理由としては、刀剣は武家にとっては命の次に大切なものであり、経済的に困っても最後まで手放さなかったことがあげられる。また日本人の間には今でも刀剣、刀装具に対する愛着が強く残っていて、愛好家が多いことも一因と思われる。

　刀剣や刀装具を作るための金工技術には、大きく分けると3つの分野がある。金属を溶かして鋳型に流し込んで成型する鋳金、金属を金槌でたたいて成形する鍛金、そして鋳金や鍛金によって成形された金属の表面を鏨で彫ったり、彫った後に異なった金属を嵌め込んだりする彫金である。

　日本の金工技術は、平安時代までは仏像や仏具を中心に発達し、武家が権力を握った鎌倉時代以降は、刀剣、刀装具、甲冑などの武具を中心に発展した。他の国々が装身具の装飾を中心に彫金技術を発展させたのと比較すると異質だ。

　日本の刀剣の歴史は弥生時代に作られた銅剣や銅矛にさかのぼる。鉄の刀剣が作られるようになったのは古墳時代、5世紀ごろといわれる。しかしそのころすでに、透かし金具や打出、線刻による金属装飾が出土品に見られる。奈良時代に入ると装飾傾向がさらに強まり、その一方で黒作と呼ばれる太刀が登場する。これは鞘が黒漆塗り、金具は鉄の簡素なもので、実用目的の太刀は装飾をほどこさないのが特徴だ。

　それが平安時代に入ると、武家が使用した兵仗用の太刀は蒔絵や螺鈿で装飾し、金具に花鳥唐草文を薄肉彫で入れたものも現れた。武家が、刀剣の装飾にこだわりを持ちはじめたことがうかがえる。

　特に武家が太刀の指添として着用した丈の短い腰刀は、室内

［125］蝶紋金総金具堆黒鞘合口拵え
正阿弥勝義作
Carved black lacquer scabbard with gold fittings
SHOAMI Katsuyoshi
長さ37.7cm

［126］裏面

［127］部分

刀装具 | 89

もふくめ常に腰に差すことからより装飾にこだわるようになった。腰刀に付ける金具には、頭、目貫、筒金、縁、小尻があり、さらに笄[註1]や小柄[註2]が加わることもある。

　こうした刀装具は、室町時代後期から太刀に代わって使われだした打刀の装飾にも用いられ、技術的に、また美術品としても目覚ましい進展を見せる。

　刀装具に最初の大きな変化が現れたのは、室町時代中期。後藤祐乗を祖とする後藤家が、赤銅[註3]を地板として表面を魚々子[註4]に仕上げ、龍や獅子などを高肉彫金色絵で表現する作風を生み出す。それは、まるで、黒漆に金高蒔絵をほどこしたかのような豪華さと品格を感じさせる作風で、後藤家はその後、幕末まで17代にわたって足利、豊臣、徳川に抱工として仕えることになる。この作風は、家彫と呼ばれ、江戸時代には改まった席では後藤家の金具を用いた拵えをするものとされた。

　次の大きな変化は色彩面での変革で、桃山時代に訪れる。さきがけとなったのが、京・西陣の埋忠明寿だった。埋忠は金、銀、素銅、真鍮、赤銅を用いた巧みな平象嵌の手法によって絵画的な鐔を生みだした。当時、打刀に付けられた鐔はほとんどが鉄製で、色金を使った鐔の出現は画期的だった。

　江戸時代に入ると本格的な戦はなくなり、平和が長く続いた。そのことが、刀装具を実戦的なものからより一層装飾的なもの、鑑賞用のものへ変化させた。

　特に江戸中期以降は、「奈良三作」と称される土屋安親、杉浦乗意、奈良利寿、町彫の祖といわれる横谷宗珉らが現れる。彼らは、肉合彫[註5]、片切彫[註6]、据文[註7]など幾多の新技法を考案し、金、銀、赤銅、素銅、真鍮、四分一[註8]といった豊富な色金を使って、色彩豊かで個性的な作品を生み出した。これらの作は、家彫に対して町彫と呼ばれた。

　技法と色金の多様さが表現力の豊かさを引き出し、他国とは比較にならないほど素晴らしい金工作品を生み出した。しかし世界に誇る日本の金工美術も、明治時代を境に衰退の一途をたどることになる。

[註]
1　笄　　　刀の横に付けて、頭や耳のかゆいところをかく。鼈甲製などは女性が髪に挿した。
2　小柄　　刀の横に付けるナイフ。ひもや紙を切る。
3　赤銅　　銅と金の合金。金は8％以下。
4　魚々子　鏨を用いて、金属の表面に付けた魚の卵のような規則正しい小さな丸の文様。
5　肉合彫　文様の輪郭を線彫りした後、内部を彫り下げて文様を描き出す彫り方。
6　片切彫　鏨を左右のどちらかに傾けて切り込む技法。傾かせ方によって陰影の深い彫り方になる。横谷宗珉が編み出した。
7　据文　　高肉象嵌の一種。高肉彫をした金属を地板に嵌め込む。
8　四分一　銅と銀の合金。

[128-131] 鶴亀図大小鐔
佐野直好作

Small and large sword guards
with crane and tortoise design
SANO Naoyoshi

[128] 鶴図表面

[129] 鶴図裏面

[130] 亀図表面

[131] 亀図裏面

刀装具 | 91

[132] 猛禽狙猿図縁頭
　　　大森英秀作
Sword collar
depicting bird of prey stalking a monkey
OMORI Teruhide

[133] 牡丹図三所物
　　　後藤光保作
Sword accessories
 (hair pick, knife handle, hilt ornament)
with peony pattern
GOTO Mitsuyasu
小柄・笄・目貫

刀装具は刀や鞘、柄につける実用、あるいは装飾用の金工品（主に）の総称である。
［133］は柄の装飾用金具である。目貫（対）と紐や紙を切るためのナイフの柄の部分である小柄と、頭皮を掻いたり耳掃除をするための道具である笄の3点セットである。

[134] 草花小禽図鐔
後藤一乗作
Sword guard with bird-and-flower design
GOTO Ichijo

[135] 裏面

[136] 茶釜図鐔
田中清寿作
Sword guard with tea kettle design
TANAKA Kiyotoshi

[137] 裏面

[138-139] 四季花鳥図大小鐔
　　　　　石黒是常作
Small and large sword guards with birds
and flowers of the four seasons
ISHIGURO Koretsune

[138] 表面

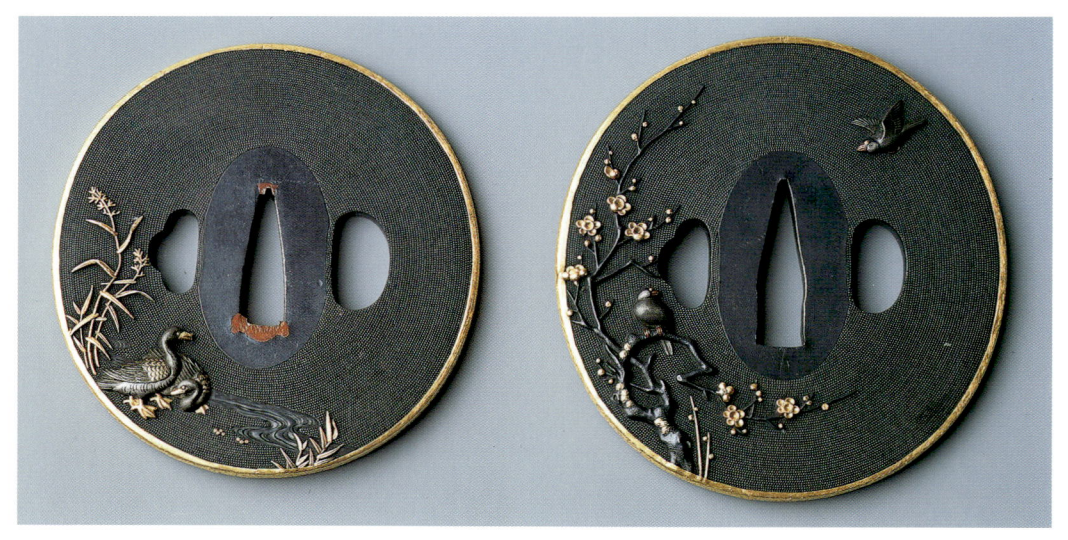

[139] 裏面

［140］群鶏図二所物
　　　石黒英明作
Knife handle and hair pick with design
of domestic fowl
ISHIGURO Hideaki

［141］小柄裏面

［142］鳳凰瑞雲図鐔
　　　三宅英光（自立軒）作
Sword guards with phoenix and clouds design
MIYAKE Terumitsu（JIRYUKEN）

［143］裏面

刀装具 | 95

[144] 蓬莱山図小柄
　　　橋本一至作
Knife handle
with depiction of Mount Horai
HASHIMOTO Isshi

[145] 粟穂図目貫
　　　荒木東明作
Hilt ornament with millet spray design
ARAKI Tomei

[146] かちかち山図目貫
　　　天光堂秀国作
Hilt Ornament depicting
the *Kachikachiyama* folk tale
TENKODO Hidekuni

［147］牡丹図鐔
中村一行常親作
Sword guard with design of peonies
NAKAMURA Ikko Tsunechika

［148］裏面

刀装具 97

[149] 吉野川図鐔
中村有宣作
Sword guard with design of Yoshino River
NAKAMURA Arinobu

[150] 裏面

[151] 月雁図鐔
青龍斎秀寿作
Sword guard with design of wild goose and the moon
SEIRYUSAI Hidetoshi

[152] 裏面

[153] 鳳凰図七宝鐔
　　　平田玄斎作
Sword guard with cloisonné of phoenix
HIRATA Gensai

[154] 裏面

[155] 胡蝶舞図小柄
　　　端信盧作
Knife handle with design depicting ancient court dance *Kochomai*
HATA Nobuyoshi

[156] 萩流水図縁頭
　　　荒井辰成作
Sword collar with design of bush clover and a rushing stream
ARAI Tatsunari

[157-161] 四季花鳥図揃金具
鈴木美彦作

Complete set of sword accessories decorated with birds and flowers of the four seasons
SUZUKI Yoshihiko

[157] 鐔　風吹牡丹図
Sword guard with windblown peonies design

[158] 裏面

昭和まで活躍した金工の名工、鈴木美彦。この三所物は美彦の代表作である。特に四分一地に金や赤銅を高肉象嵌した風吹牡丹図の鐔は、幕末・明治の名工に優るとも劣らない技量を発揮した作品である。

[159] 目貫　春秋花鳥図
Hilt decoration depicting spring and autumn birds (bush warbler and quail)

[160] 小柄　雪中鷺図
Knife handle with design of heron in the snow

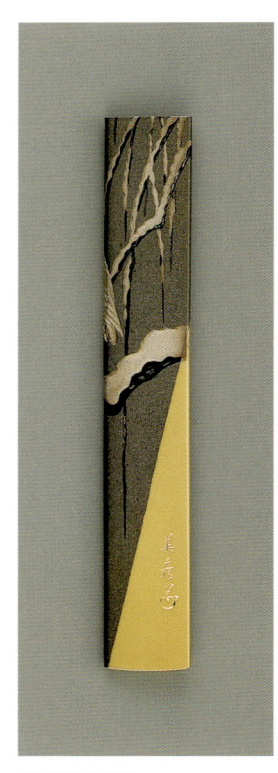

[161] 裏面

[162] 蓮図鐔
　　　加納夏雄作
Sword guard with lotus design
KANO Natsuo

[163] 裏面

広い空間を残した独特の表現は夏雄の特徴の一つといえる。その空間に鏨でつけられた地模様と、間によって生まれる品格は、他の追随を許さない。

[164] アイリス図鐔
　　　加納夏雄作
Sword guard with iris design
KANO Natsuo

[165] 裏面

刀装具 | 101

金工
きんこう

Metalwork

　1868年、250年以上続いた幕藩体制は崩壊し、明治政府が生まれた。工芸で一番大きな影響を受けたのは金工の分野だった。それまで将軍家や大名家をパトロンとして生計を立てていた刀装金工たちは、武士階級の消滅とそれに続く明治9（1876）年の廃刀令施行により突然、生活の糧を失うことになる。

　鐔などの刀装金具は、純粋に美術品として多少の需要はあったが、微々たる量で、生活を維持できるような水準ではなかった。

　彼らは、刀装金具の加工で培った高い技術を他の分野で生かすべく、模索せざるを得なかった。そして、帯留め、煙草入れの金具、輸出向けの置物や花瓶、皿、香炉、煙草箱などの製作に活路を見いだした。

　一方、明治政府は、国力を高めるために殖産興業政策を推し進めていった。当時の開国まもない日本には工業製品と呼べるものはなく、唯一、貿易用に輸出できたのは手作りの伝統的工芸品だけだった。政府がそうしたなかで目を向けたものの一つが、失業の憂き目にあっていた金工分野だった。

　日本が国家として初めて公式に参加した明治6（1873）年のウィーン万国博覧会で、金工をはじめ日本の工芸品は爆発的な人気を博した。連日、日本館は押すな押すなの大盛況だったという。それまで日本の工芸品は、オランダなどを通じて蒔絵や磁器類が多少ヨーロッパに知られていた。しかし本格的な紹介はこの時が初めてだった。日本政府はその後も継続して万博に出展し、日本の、特に金工作品に対する称賛の声は大きかったという。

　当時、欧米諸国で作られていた金工作品はブロンズや銀の鋳造品が多く、日本のように金、銀、素銅、赤銅、四分一といった多様な色金を用いて、高度な彫りや複雑な象嵌技術で加工したものは皆無だった。万博会場では、展示だけでなく販売もしてい

[166] 群鶏図香炉
正阿弥勝義作
Incense burner with domestic fowls
SHOAMI Katsuyoshi
高さ15cm

[167] 部分

勝義は中央に出ていれば、まちがいなく帝室技芸員になっていた名工である。岡山藩お抱えの金工であった勝義は、細部にいたるまで手抜きをしない作品作り、高度な技術、高い独創性で、海外にもファンは多い。

たため、飛ぶような売れゆきだったという。

　こうした優れた工芸美術を継承、発展させるため、政府は明治23（1890）年、帝室技芸員制度を設けた。帝室技芸員に選ばれると、皇室や宮内省（現、宮内庁）から相当の仕事の依頼を受け、生活は安定し社会的地位も高まった。同じころに東京美術学校も授業を開始した。帝室技芸員に選ばれた金工分野の第一人者、加納夏雄（1828-98）は、東京美術学校彫金科の初代教授にも就き、後進を指導した。このことは金工を志す人たちにとって大きな励みになった。

　その後、金工分野の帝室技芸員には、海野勝珉（1844-1915）、香川勝広（1853-1917）、塚田秀鏡（1848-1918）といった明治を代表する彫金の名工たちが任命された。帝室技芸員には選ばれなかったが、彼ら以上の力量があった正阿弥勝義（1832-1908）のことも忘れてはならない。

　明治という時代は、金工を志した人たちにとって波乱の時代であった。しかし彼らは、武家社会の崩壊、開国、国際化、といった激流に翻弄されながらも、そのなかで刀装金工の技術を生かして、色彩感のある絵画的な表現で世界に類のない美術品を創り出した。明治の金工たちの努力と才覚に賛辞を惜しまない。

[168] 龍虎図花瓶　一対
海野勝珉作
Pair of vases with tiger and dragon
UNNO Shomin
高さ38cm

勝義・夏雄と並んで明治を代表する名工である勝珉は特に立体的な表現が得意であった。この作品は大正3年の大正博覧会に出品された作品であるが、朧銀(銅と銀の合金)地を鋤彫りし、金の平象嵌、高肉象嵌をほどこして迫力ある龍虎を表現している。

金工 | 105

[169] 雀かたばみ図煙草ケース
　　　海野勝珉作
Cigarette case with sparrows and wood sorrel
UNNO Shomin
長辺15.0cm

[170] 孔雀図宝石箱
　　　飴谷有珉作
Jewelry box with peacock
AMETANI Yumin
長辺20.0cm

[171] 紅葉桜図香合
　　　正阿弥勝義作
Incense container with maple
leaves and cherry blossoms
SHOAMI Katsuyoshi
径7.0cm

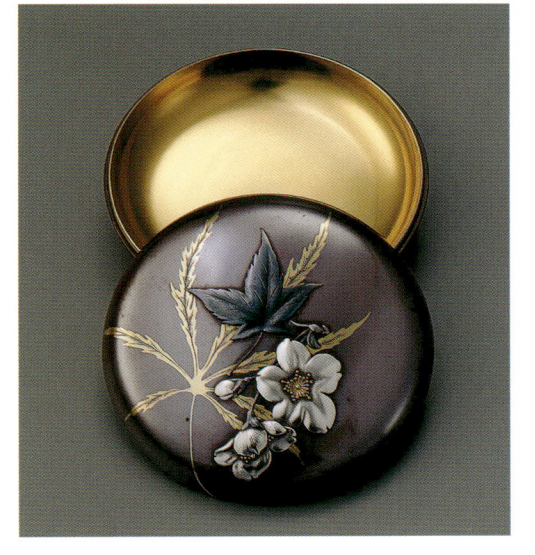

[172] 芍薬図懐中時計蓋
　　　加納夏雄作
Watchcase with peony
KANO Natsuo
径6.0cm

勝義の香合には名品が多い。この香合の蓋には緋銅が使われている。緋銅は扱いが難しくめったに使われることはないが、勝義はその緋銅に金の平象嵌で細葉紅葉を、赤銅の高肉象嵌で紅葉を、そして金、銀の高肉象嵌で桜花を表現している(左)。
金、銀の平象嵌で芍薬花を入れた後、片切彫で枝葉を表現した夏雄らしい作品。夏雄の片切彫には他の人に真似できない切れの良さと味がある(右)。

雪峰英友についてはよくわかっていないが、その作風は正阿弥勝義の作品と共通しているものがある。なかなかの名工である。銀地から菊を彫り出して金象嵌している。

[173] 押合菊香合
　　　大森雪峰英友作
Incense container with relief chrysanthemums
OMORI Seppo Hidetomo
高さ8.0cm

帝室技芸員クラスの名工の金工作品が世界各国の万国博覧会で受賞を重ね、欧米の美術館やコレクターたちに買い取られ、宮内省に買い上げられて来日の要人への献上品になっていった。その一方で、多くの無名の刀装金工の作品も、嘱品家を通じて輸出され、海外のコレクターたちの需要を満たしていった。

　日本が国家として初めて参加した明治6（1873）年のウィーン万国博覧会を境に、多くの嘱品家が生まれた。嘱品家とは、製造部門を持たず、作品の制作を工人に委嘱し、自らの名で万博に出品したり直接輸出を手がける商人や会社のことをいう。起立工商会社、金沢銅器会社、大関弥兵衛などが活躍した。横浜に店を持ち、外国人を相手に商売をし、なかには海外に支店を持って貿易をする会社もあった。

　そのなかで、起立工商会社は、もともと政府の万博参加に際して出品された大量の作品を現地で売却するのを目的に設立された一種の国策会社でもあった。ニューヨーク、パリに支店を持ち、明治13（1880）年の時点で従業員が43人いたといわれている。

　起立工商会社は一流の工人に作品を委嘱したが、作品の装飾や形は下図工にデザインさせていた。明治24（1891）年に解散することになるが、半官半民だったためか市場ニーズの把握に疎く、他の民間の嘱品家に比べて随分早い時期の解散であった。その際パリやニューヨークにあった資産の売却を試みたが、流行遅れの様式のため難航したという。

　金沢銅器会社は明治10（1877）年、金工職人の救済と新しい金工品の海外輸出を目的に、石川県金沢区長町に設立された。参画した工人のなかには、水野源六光春（1838-95）、山川孝次（1828-82）ら金沢の名工が並んでいた。

　超高級金工作品の嘱品家として欧米で人気が高かったのは、大関弥兵衛であった。大関が制作を委嘱した工人には、海野盛寿、山田元信、兼康正寿、池田民国といった名工が数多くいたが、万博などへは「大関」のブランド名で出品した。

　大関の作品は、非常に高度な象嵌技術を駆使して見る人を驚かせるが、日本人からすると装飾過剰のように見える。しかしそれは、逆にいえば、彼らが欧米人の好みを的確に把握し、事業家として成功したことの証でもあるといえる。大関は、大正期まで活動を続けていたようだ。

　金工作品を手がける会社のなかには、制作委嘱だけではなく、実際に製造部門を持つ会社もあった。そのなかで最も注目すべき存在は京都の駒井と紹美であろう。

　駒井は天保12（1841）年に駒井清兵衛が創業したといわれているが、有名な金銀の布目象嵌の作品を作りはじめたのは、初代駒井音次郎（1842-1917）になってからである。

[174] 鷺図花瓶　一対
香川勝広作
Pair of vases with herons
KAGAWA Katsuhiro
高さ38.0cm

音次郎は13歳のころ、肥後出身の刀装金工、三崎周助から象嵌技法を学ぶ機会を得た。明治9 (1876) 年の廃刀令まで刀装金具を作っていたが、明治6年ごろから外国人向けの置物や飾り物も手がけるようになる。
　駒井の繊細で緻密な作品は欧米でたちまち人気を呼び、京都でも類似の品を製造する業者が出てきた。駒井は昭和16 (1941) 年まで金工作品を作り続ける。
　紹美も駒井と並んで海外で成功した製造業者だ。紹美栄祐は、9代金谷五郎三郎のもとで金工を学んだとされ、国内外のさまざまな博覧会に出品した。中級品と高級品を作り分け、中級品の工房だけでも81ヶ所に持っていたことが知られている。単純に見積もっても数百人にのぼる数の元刀装金工たちを雇っていたことになる。
　このように、明治初期には数多くの嘱品家や製造業者が現れ、多くは欧米人たちの好みを的確に把握して、多くの刀装金工たちの生活の糧を生み出したのである。今でも、ニューヨークやロンドンの日本美術品のオークションでは、必ずといってよいほど駒井や紹美の作品が並ぶ。大関の作品が出ると、オークションルームは過熱し、1千万円、2千万円という高値がつくのである。

[175] 牡丹雀図一輪挿し
小林親光作
Bud vase with peony and sparrow
KOBAYASHI Chikamitsu
高さ22.0cm

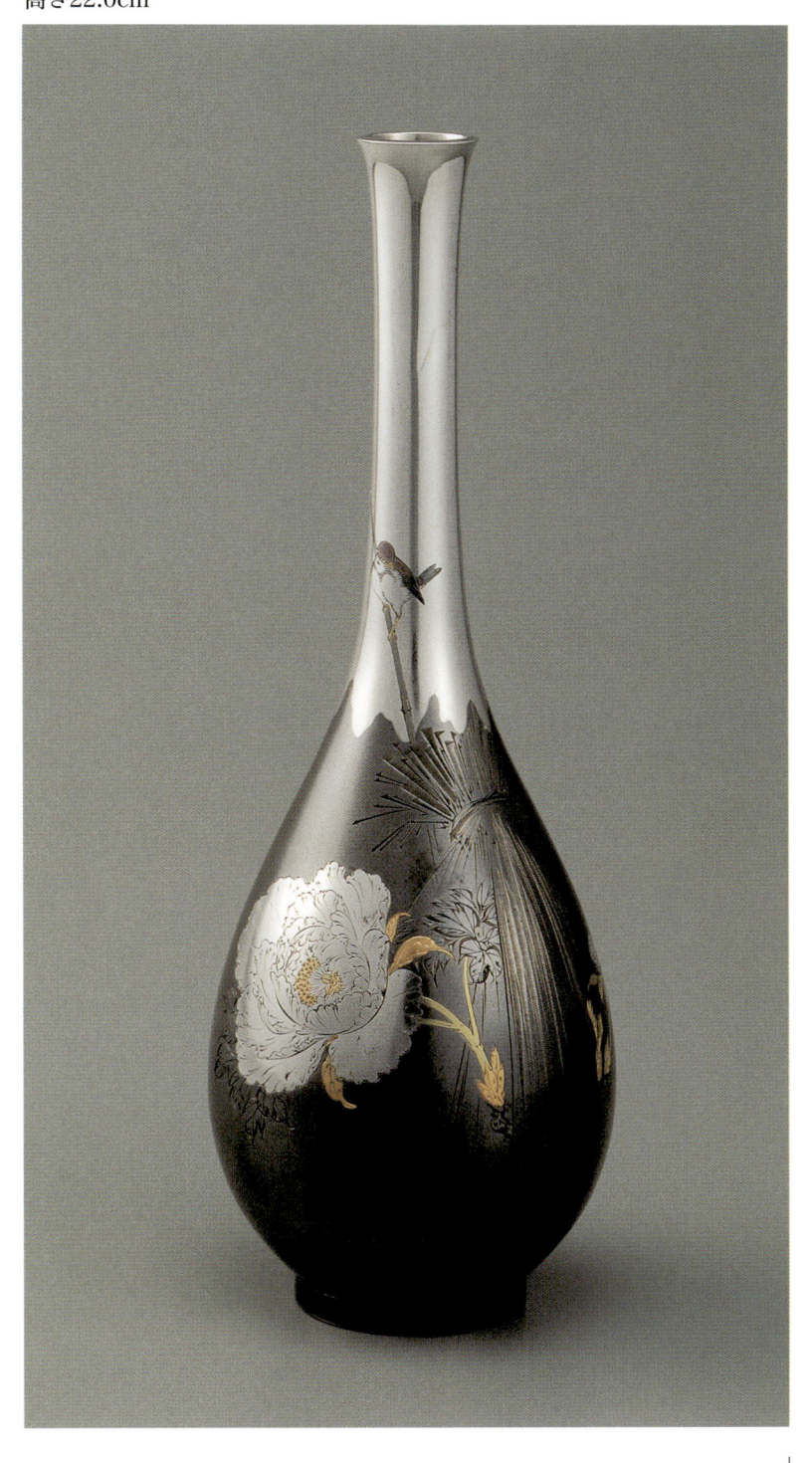

[176] 菊図花瓶
高玉斎一久作
Vase with chrysanthemums
KOGYOKUSAI Ikkyu
高さ30.0cm

この一輪挿しは首の部分で四分一銀と銀を接合している。複雑な曲線に切って接合するには高度な技術と熟練が必要とされる。

［177］桜雉図花瓶
　　　佐藤秀広作
Vase with cherry blossoms and pheasants
SATO Hidehiro
高さ30.0cm

［178］市井図香炉
　　　海野盛寿（凌雲斎）作
Incense burner with well-side scene
UNNO Moritoshi(RYOUNSAI)
高さ15.0cm

［179］草花図金象嵌銀製香炉
　　　無銘
Silver incense burner with
overlay gold areas in floral design
No signature
高さ15.0cm

［180］古代文唐草象嵌香炉
無銘
Incense burner with inlaid ancient-style
Chinese arabesque pattern
No signature
高さ25.0cm

[181] 草花文布目象嵌香炉
　　　駒井製
Incense burner with inlaid floral designs in textured panels
KOMAI workshop
高さ29.0cm

鉄地に本象嵌と布目象嵌が施された見事な作品。作風から幕末・明治に活躍した鹿島一谷のものと思われる。鹿島一谷は布目象嵌の名工であった。

［182］花鳥図鉄地布目象嵌香炉
鹿島一谷作

Iron incense burner with textured panels depicting birds and flowers
KAJIMA Ikkoku

高さ25.0cm

蒔絵
まきえ

Lacquer

　日本の工芸品のなかで最も早い時期に海外へ流出していったものは蒔絵である。
　天文18（1549）年、宣教師フランシスコ・ザビエルが鹿児島に上陸してキリスト教がわが国にもたらされ、その後急速に全国に広まる。来日した多くのイエズス会宣教師たちは、黄金色に美しく輝く蒔絵漆器に魅せられ、彼らの祭儀具を螺鈿などを配した蒔絵で装飾することを思いつく。聖龕（聖人たちの姿を描いた絵の入れ物）、ミサで分かつパンの器・聖餅箱、聖書を載せる書見台などである。彼らはおびただしい数の祭儀具を、当時、高台寺蒔絵を製造していたであろう京都の職人たちに直接発注したという。
　宣教師たちが発注し、本国に送り込んだこれらの蒔絵祭儀具は本国でも大評判となり、当時来日した東インド会社の商人も蒔絵をヨーロッパへ輸出するようになる。彼らもまた京都の蒔絵師たちに直接注文したようだ。
　当時、蒔絵生産の中心地は京都だった。彼らが好んで発注したのは、洋櫃、書簞笥、飾り箱などで、「南蛮漆器」の製作は京都の一大産業になったと考えられる。今でもロンドンやニューヨークの日本美術のオークションでは、そのころの蒔絵作品がしばしば登場する。また、ヨーロッパの各地の美術館にも、桃山・江戸時代初めの蒔絵作品が数多く所蔵されている。
　このように盛んに製造、輸出された南蛮漆器も、徳川幕府が鎖国政策をとることによって状況は一変する。寛永16（1639）年、幕府はオランダ一国との交流を決め、スペインやポルトガルの宣教師との交流を途絶えさせた。南蛮漆器の輸出も、これによって終焉を迎えることになる。とはいっても、漆器類の輸出そのものがなくなったわけではなかった。オランダの貿易商たちは唯一の

[183] 十香図蒔絵文庫
川之辺一朝作
Letter box with maki-e design of fragrant flowers
KAWANOBE Itcho
縦42.0cm　横34.5cm　高さ16.0cm

［184］裏面

貿易港、長崎・出島を通じて大量の蒔絵類を日本から運び出したのである。

そのようにしてヨーロッパに渡った蒔絵類のなかで特に有名なのは、フランス国王ルイ16世の王妃マリー・アントワネット（1755-93）の小箱のコレクションだ。マリー・アントワネットは、フランス革命のさなかギロチンで処刑された悲劇の主人公。

彼女が所有した小箱類中心の蒔絵大コレクションは現在、ヴェルサイユ宮殿、ルーブル美術館、ギメ美術館に分散して保管されている。コレクションが、はたしてマリー・アントワネット自身によって集められたものなのか、それとも母親であるオーストリア女帝マリア・テレジアが集めたものかは定かではないが、これらの蒔絵小箱がオランダ商人の手を経て出島からヨーロッパに渡ったことだけはまちがいない。

こうして桃山・江戸時代に輸出され続けた日本の蒔絵類の美しさ

［185-186］
散り紅葉図蒔絵板文庫
池田泰真作
Wood letter box with pattern of falling autumn foliage in maki-e relief
IKEDA Taishin
縦26.0cm　横21.0cm

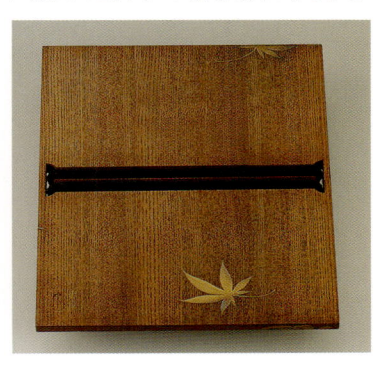

は、幕末に日本が開国する以前から、ヨーロッパの上流階級の間では知れ渡っていた。明治6（1873）年、明治政府が初めてウィーン万国博覧会に参加すると、日本の蒔絵は高い評価を得、それ以後、日本の蒔絵類は国内に残っていた質の高いものを中心に急速に海外へ流出していく。

一方、明治の新作蒔絵は、海外の需要を意識した器形や意匠による作品が東京・横浜を中心に作られ、最初はそれなりの成功は収めたものの、粗製濫造品が出まわったり、意匠のマンネリ化などが進んで海外市場での評価を落とすことになった。

この状況に危機感を抱いた漆工業界は明治24（1891）年、日本漆工会を設立、業界の建て直しをはかる。明治政府も明治22年、東京美術学校の設立に当たって、漆工技術の継承と向上を目的とする漆工科を設置した。後進を指導したのは、川之辺一朝（1830-1910）、池田泰真（1825-1903）、白山松哉（1853-1923）といった明治を代表する名工や帝室技芸員たちで、常に日本の漆工芸の水準を高めてきた人たちだった。

蒔絵は漆器の装飾技法の一つで、日本で独自に生まれたものである。中国や朝鮮半島にも存在しない。平安時代にはすでに

蒔絵 | 121

基本的な技法が完成されていて、それ以前から存在していたと考えられている。

　蒔絵を簡単に説明すると、漆器製造の最終工程で生漆を用いて絵や文様を描き、その上に金粉や銀粉を蒔いて漆が乾きやすいように温度や湿度を設定した空間（風呂という）に入れて乾燥させる。漆が乾いた後に表面をキメの細かい炭で研いで完成させる。

　実際の工程はもっと複雑多様で、特に高蒔絵や研出し蒔絵は、工程が多く、熟練した高度な技を必要とする。時代とともに進化をとげた蒔絵技法は、幕末・明治期にその頂点に達した。

　江戸時代、蒔絵が一番盛んであったのは京都、江戸、金沢だった。その後、東京への遷都や明治政府の輸出重視政策によって三都市間の生産のバランスが崩れた。東京は横浜に近いこともあって、輸出用蒔絵を多く生産し、京都や金沢は量で東京に水をあけられることになる。その一方、東京では粗悪品も多く出まわって評価を落とす弊害もあった。その点、京都や金沢では、伝統の技を重視した堅実な蒔絵が多く作られた。

　明治期に、東京や横浜の輸出用蒔絵によく使われた加飾技法に、芝山細工と杣田細工がある。いずれも幕末になって新たに生まれた技法で、国内向けの漆器にはほとんど使われることはなかった。

　芝山細工は、漆器や象牙などの器物の上に象牙、貝、珊瑚、鼈甲などをいろいろな形に細工して象嵌した後、残った空間を蒔絵で装飾する技法。上総の国芝山（千葉県中北部）の大野木専蔵が考案したという。

　杣田細工は、アワビの薄貝を細かに切り、同様に細かく切った金の薄板とともに漆器の上に貼り付けていく緻密な細工だ。京都から富山藩に招かれた杣田清輔によって始められた。

　芝山細工や杣田細工に使われている、象牙や鼈甲、青貝や金

[187] 籬秋草蒔絵木瓜形小箱
芝舩作
Small box with maki-e design of bamboo fence and autumn plants
Signed "SHISEN"
縦8.0cm　横8.0cm　高さ3.7cm

の切片を貼り付ける技法は、それ以前の蒔絵にも部分的に使われていたが、あくまでも蒔絵が主で象嵌や貼り付けは従であった。それが芝山や杣田では主従が逆転する。そして、これらの加飾をほどこした蒔絵は海外で大評判となり、大量に製作されることになる。

芝山と杣田に共通しているは、色彩の華やかさ、仕事の緻密さ、細密さだ。従来の蒔絵はほとんどが、金一色の金蒔絵か、黒地に金蒔絵をほどこした地黒(じぐろ)蒔絵であった。

芝山の場合、金地に赤、オレンジ、緑、青、茶などの華やかな色彩をちりばめ、杣田の場合は、アワビ貝のグリーン、ピンク、ブルーの部分からそれぞれ細片を作り、金の薄板の切片と組み合わせて黒漆の上に美しい絵を描き出す。

両者が欧米で高い評価を受けたのは充分納得できるし、むしろ、日本でこれらの技法を使った作品がなぜもっと作られなかったのか不思議なくらい魅力を感じる。明治という時代はいろいろ試行錯誤を繰り返しながらも、蒔絵の世界においては活気のある楽しい時代だった。

[188] 猫孔雀羽根図蒔絵入れ子小箱（内箱　闘鶏図）
無銘

Inset box set, outer box with maki-e depiction of
cat playing with peacock feathers,
two inner boxes decorated with fighting cocks
No signature

縦8.0cm　横10.5cm　高さ3.5cm

［189］花尽くし図蒔絵重小箱
　　　　飯塚桃葉作
Set of stacking boxes with maki-e floral designs
IIZUKA Toyo
縦9.5cm　横9.0cm　高さ10.5cm

［190］重小箱内側

［191］撫子図蒔絵小箱
　　　　無銘
Small box with maki-e wild carnations
No signature
縦10.0cm　横11.0cm　高さ5.5cm

[192] 宇治川先陣図蒔絵小箱
沢田宗沢斎作
Small box with maki-e depiction of
the attack on Uji River
SAWADA Sotakusai
縦12.0cm　横15.0cm　高さ6.5cm

[193] 小箱蓋裏

[194] 渦文蒔絵香合
　　　白山松哉作
Incense container with ripple pattern
SHIRAYAMA Shosai
径9.0cm　高さ2.0cm

　　　白山松哉は高度な技法と気品のある作風で東京美術学校初代漆芸科教授になっ
　　た人である。粘度の強い漆で同じ太さの細線を連続して描くことは至難の技で
　　ある。それを同じ間隔で渦巻きに仕上げるのはさらに難しい。白山松哉は帝室技
　　芸員としても活躍した。

[195] 菊文蒔絵棗
白山松哉作
Tea container with maki-e
chrysanthemum pattern
SHIRAYAMA Shosai
径5.0cm　高さ6.0cm

[196] 菊文蒔絵香合
白山松哉作
Incense container with maki-e
chrysanthemum pattern
SHIRAYAMA Shosai
径7.5cm　高さ2.0cm

蒔絵 | 127

[197-198] 日月烏鷺図蒔絵額　一対
　　　　　白山松哉作
Pair of lacquer plaques, sun and herons (left), moon and crow (right)
SHIRAYAMA Shosai
縦78.5cm　横36.0cm

[198]

蒔絵 129

[199] 花尽くし図蒔絵香箱
無銘
Incense box with maki-e floral design
No signature
縦12.0cm　横9.0cm　高さ4.0cm

[200] 蓋と内部

[201] 乗合船図蒔絵硯箱
無銘
Writing box with maki-e depiction of a ferry boat
No signature
縦24.0cm　横22.5cm　高さ4.5cm

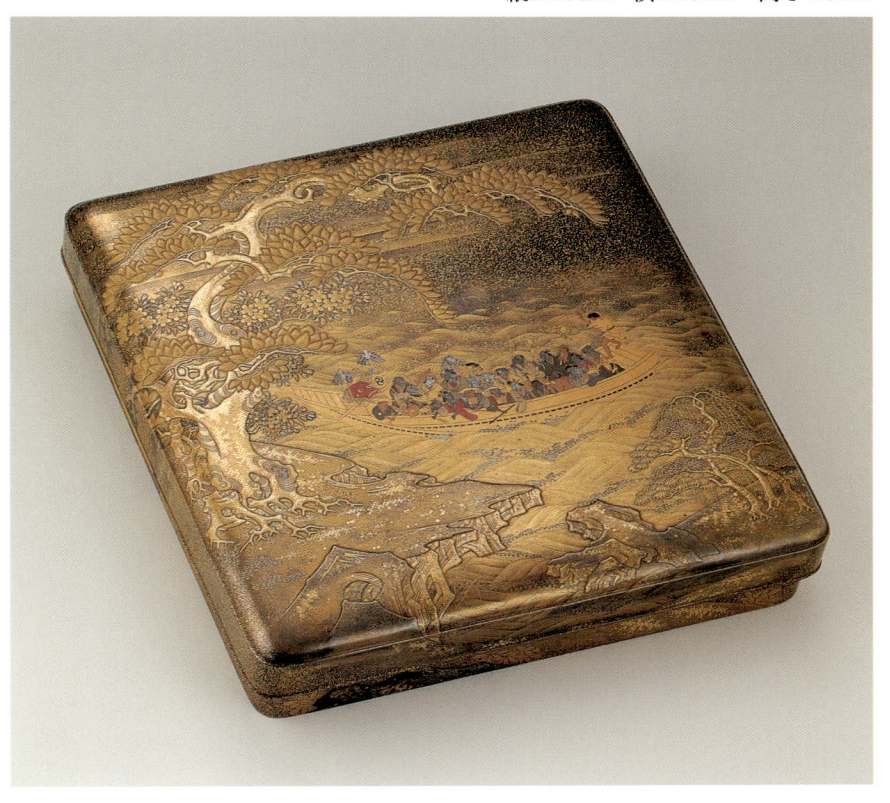

[202] 蓋裏と内部

［203］桜樹下鶏図小箱
　　　杣田細工
Small box with cock beneath a cherry tree
SOMADA style
縦5.2cm　横8.0cm　高さ2.0cm

［204］狐の嫁入り図入れ子小箱
　　　杣田細工
Inset box set with depiction of foxes' wedding
SOMADA style
縦6.0cm　横10.0cm　高さ5.0cm

［205］内部

芝山細工や杣田細工は輸出用の小箱等の加飾技法としてよく使われた。カラフルで派手なところが欧米人のテイストに合ったのであろう。杣田細工はスナッフボトルの装飾にも使われ、中国にも輸出されていた。

［206］花雉図蒔絵小箱
芝山細工
Small box with maki-e depiction of flowers and pheasant
SHIBAYAMA style
縦11.0cm　横9.0cm　高さ4.5cm

［207］蓋裏と内部

[209] 裏面

　この作品は蒔絵のあらゆる技法を駆使して作られた赤塚自得の最高傑作の一つである。この作品は大正3年の大正博に出品され、その時の総裁をつとめた閑院宮に献上された。
　赤塚自得は帝室技芸員としても活躍し、宮内省の注文で多くの御下賜用の作品を作ったことでも知られている。

[208] 四季草花図蒔絵提簞笥
赤塚自得作
Portable chest with maki-e depiction of
flowers of the four seasons
AKATSUKA Jitoku
縦15.9cm　横24.3cm　高さ22.5cm

評価される細密工芸
幕末・明治の工芸美術

原田一敏〈東京国立博物館 上席研究員〉

Important Craft Objects of
the Late Edo and Meiji Periods
Kazutoshi Harada

　日本はアジアのもっとも東にあって、古代から美術や工芸は中国や朝鮮半島の影響を受けていたが、その逆として、日本の美術工芸が、海外に輸出され、そして評価されるようになったのはいつごろからであろうか。少なくとも、早くから交渉のあった中国や朝鮮半島などでは、高い評価を受けたという証としての、日本美術工芸品が模倣(もほう)されるというようなことは、あまり事例を聞かない。では貿易品として、外国ではどのようなものに人気があったのであろうか。

　応永8（1401）年、足利義満が遣明船を派遣し、以後足利将軍家を中心に行なわれた日明貿易では、日本から輸出された主要な美術品といえるものは、蒔絵(まきえ)漆器と扇であった。これらの中国での評価というものは具体的には伝わっていないが、扇に関しては応仁2（1468）年に入明した際の記録では、「一、黒地上ニ竜蒔絵、御扇百本入皆エリホ子（ネ）。代廿三貫八百五十文」（『戊子入明記』）とあり、黒漆塗りに金蒔絵で竜を表わした箱に、扇が百本入っていたとある。さらに宝徳3（1451）年出航船には、1350本もの扇が舶載された状況であった。当然のことながら中国でも扇は作られていたが、これだけの数が輸出されたという事実は、これらの扇に魅力的な要素があったからであろう。具体的にこの扇がどのようなものであったかは記述されていないが、現存している遺品から想像すると、南北朝時代最末期の明徳2（1391）年に調進された熊野速玉神社(くまのはやたま)の古神宝の扇にみるような、樹や花鳥文様が描かれていたのかもしれない。また天文8（1539）年に策彦(さくげん)周良(しゅうりょう)が入明した時、狩野元信の画いた扇面を持っていったところ、鄭沢(ていたく)という僧が大いに称したとある（『古画備考』）。

江戸期の評価

　さて、ここで述べる細密工芸というと、それは工芸品のなかでも小さな作品であり、しかも技術としては細密でなおかつ精巧であるもの、と概念としていえるものであろう。小さくても技術的に雑な造形、文様表現をしているものは当然ふくまれない。この細

密精巧な工芸品を作る感覚、技術は、日本ほど卓越した国は、ほとんどないといえるであろう。中国においても、唐時代の銀器や明清時代のかぎ煙草入れ、玉や象牙の彫刻には非常に精巧な技術が見られるが、日本の特に江戸時代から明治時代にかけての金工、漆工、陶磁、木牙彫のあらゆる分野で展開された超絶ともいうべき細密精巧な世界は、他国にも例を見ない。そうした工芸品は日常で使用されていたものであり、当時の人々も当然のように使用していたのであるが、美術作品としてそれを評価し、コレクションという形で評価したのはヨーロッパの人々であった。

その早い時期のコレクターの一人はフランス王ルイ16世の妃マリー・アントワネット（1755-93）であろう。マリー・アントワネットのコレクションは、江戸時代18世紀の蒔絵の小箱が中心で、瓜、犬、鶏などの形をした蓋物や、太鼓や籠をかたどって、その箱の中にさらに小さな箱を5個6個と入れたものであり、この小箱の中には宝石を入れていたと伝えている。

日本の蒔絵がヨーロッパに輸出されたのは16世紀末期、ポルトガルやスペイン船によるのが早いと考えられている。それらの多くは日本では、かつて南蛮漆器と呼ばれていた黒漆地に、花鳥文様を蒔絵で表わし、螺鈿を加えたもので、洋櫃、箪笥、聖龕などキリスト教会で用いられた宗教用具や貴族の邸宅に置かれた家具類などであった。これらはヨーロッパ中に広く賞用されたことは、今も各地の宮殿の室内装飾として伝えられていることでも理解できよう。17世紀にはいるとオランダ人ヤン・ヨースティン、イギリス人ウイリアム・アダムスらが、日本との交易が有望であるとの見通しによって、1609年にはオランダ、1613年にはイギリスが平戸に商館を開設し、本格的な貿易が開始された。彼らによって日本から輸出された文物は、ウイリアム・アダムスの書簡集『慶元イギリス書簡』から見てみると、銅や鉄といった金属素材、また製品では扇、傘、蒔絵、所帯道具、塗り物などであり、日本に輸入されたものは羅紗や緞子など染織品が多かったようである。

ではこのような細密な工芸品がどのようにして作られるようになったか、一例をあげて考えてみよう。

江戸時代もっとも発達した工芸に装剣金具がある。装剣金工は、日本刀の外装に取り付けられた金具であるが、武士が太刀に代わって刀と脇差を帯に差すようになって、それまでの太刀の形式的であった外装金具からさまざまな文様を多彩な金属を使用して、いろいろな技法を併用して表わすようになった。その先駆的な工人が慶長から寛永のころ、京都西陣に住した埋忠明寿であった。明寿の作品は鐔だけであるが、使用している金属は、金、銀、素銅、真鍮で、赤銅の鐔の地に金、銀、素銅を用いて平象嵌の技法で葡

萄胡蝶や蔦を絵画的に表わしたり、あるいは同じ葡萄文でも真鍮を地板として、金、銀、素銅による平象嵌をほどこしたものなどであった。室町時代後期から桃山時代にかけて太刀に代わって用いられた打刀に付けられた鐔は、鉄製がほとんどであったと思われるが、この明寿の色彩感のある鐔の出現は、江戸の装剣金工に始まり、明治の輸出金工にいたるまで、表現法としてその根底を支えるものであった。江戸時代には平象嵌から、さらに文様を肉高、立体的に表現するようになり、高肉象嵌、布目象嵌、色絵といった色彩感を出す技法、また肉合彫、片切彫といった文様を彫刻で表わす技法までが開発された。明治時代にヨーロッパ、アメリカで開催された万国博覧会に出品され、絶賛された日本金工の技術的な基礎は、これら装剣金工に拠るものといっても過言ではないであろう。

　また、現在も人気が高い印籠、それに付属する根付や緒締めであるが、これも装身具として必要欠くべからざるものとして、大量に作られていた。この大量に作られたことが、技術の向上、新たな技法の開発へと展開してゆき、今日高く評価され、そして数が多いからこそコレクションの対象となったのである。

明治期の評価

　明治時代に入ると、日本美術工芸は、欧米でコレクションという形で高い評価を受けるようになる。評価されるようになったその主要な要因は、万国博覧会に日本の美術工芸品が展示され、広く知れ渡ったことであろう。日本が万国博覧会に初出品したのは、慶応3（1867）年のパリが最初であり、その後、明治6（1873）年のウィーン、明治9（1876）年のフィラデルフィア、明治11（1878）年のパリ、明治22（1889）年のパリ、明治26（1893）年のシカゴ、明治33（1900）年パリなどと立て続けに参加することとなる。博覧会の評価が、直接日本美術の輸出すなわち外貨の獲得となるわけであり、国策として欧米人の好む傾向が研究された。美術商の林忠正、工芸教育家で図案家の納富介次郎、画家の浅井忠などがその傾向と対策を研究していたことはよく知られている。

　博覧会のことは、本書ヴィクター・ハリス氏の論文に詳しいので、ここでは述べないが、内容について触れておきたい。

　初めて参加した慶応3年のパリ万博は、博覧会用として作品を制作したのではなく、既存の実用品として使用されていた工芸品を選択して出品したものであり、輸出商品としての認識はなった。しかし明治9年からは博覧会出品物として制作されるようになる。金工では、蠟型鋳造による過剰ともいえる装飾をほどこした大型の銅製花瓶、香炉であり、また小さなものでは、花瓶や水盤、香炉で、花鳥文様を各種の金属を用いて高肉象嵌をしたもので、色彩

を意識した作品が目立っている。また陶磁も、薩摩焼、香蘭社、宮川香山などによる細密な色絵をほどこしたものや、有田や瀬戸の染付の大型の燈籠や飾り皿が主要なものであった。漆工では明治6年のウィーン万博では幕末期の棚や小簞笥、香箱、短冊箱、香合などを出品していたが、明治9年のフィラデルフィアからは柴田是真、池田泰真、川之辺一朝らの名工による蒔絵と色漆による日本的な風物を描いた額が多くなる。絵画に通ずる鑑賞用の工芸作品を展示するという傾向は、明治26年のシカゴ万博でピークに達する。

明治前期の万博参加の目的の第一は殖産興業であったが、シカゴ博覧会では、工芸品をふくめた日本美術全体が、万博内の美術館に飾るにふさわしい「美術（アート）」として認められることが大きな目的と認識されていた。このことは日本が世界に比して一等国である証でもあった。万博敷地内には、工芸館と美術館があったが、美術館での陳列は彫刻、絵画、装飾美術（これをさらに金工、陶磁、漆工などに分類する）などいくつかの部門に分けられていて、米国側の見解として、材質にかぎらず、色、図ともに絵画的表現を行っているものも広く絵画作品とみなすとして、絵画すなわち美術館に陳列されるようになった。これを受けて、金工では加納夏雄、海野勝珉などは色金を多用した象嵌の額を作り、陶磁では花瓶という形をとって、そこに花鳥文様あるいは日本の風景を染付や色絵で表わし、また漆工も江ノ島図額（池田泰真）といった額が制作されるにいたった。また染織でも西村治兵衛の花鳥図屏風、田中利七の孔雀図屏風、川島甚兵衛の花鳥図壁掛は染織という技法による絵画作品といえるような作風を示すものであった。

このシカゴ博覧会の出品作で特筆されるのは、金工の鈴木長吉作の「十二羽の鷹」［挿図1］で、シカゴのみならず米国諸州の新聞に、その姿態の多様さ、合金の発色の美しさで絶賛され、「我カ美術館ノタメニ光彩を添ユルモノナリ」との美術部長アンヴィス氏の言葉を載せている。このような日本金工について日本側も臨時博覧会事務局の報告では、「外国の日本の長技とするところは殊に繊細巧緻にあって、外国は専ら偉大豪壮を主としており、多くはブロンズの鋳像であり、巧妙な象嵌や色の配色を合金に求めたものはない」としている。まさに金工のみならず、陶磁、漆工、染織、七宝にいたるまでの日本工芸の特質は、細緻であるということ、そして色彩感にあったのである。

ところで、こうしてたびたび開かれた万国博覧会であるが、現在も欧米で人気の高い印籠、根付、装剣金具の本格的な出品はほとんど見当たらないのである。それはおそらく、博覧会という公的

［挿図1］
鈴木長吉作「十二羽の鷹」の内4羽
東京国立近代美術館蔵
『万国博覧会の美術』展カタログより転載

評価される細密工芸

な場で紹介されるまでもなく、すでに個人のコレクションという形で高く評価することが浸透していたと推測される。とくに1850年代から台頭したジャポニスムの思潮のなかで、来日した欧米人がこれらを買い求めて本国に送るようになり、それらの研究も盛んになった。1881年には、根付に関連してエドモンド・デ・コンコルトがチェリーニ（ルネサンス期のフィレンツェの彫刻家で金・銀細工師）の名を引き合いに出して紹介し、1883年にはルイス・ゴンスが刀の鐔について著作し、1881-91年にかけてS.ビンガが『LE JAPON ARTISTIQUE』というタイトルの日本美術全般にわたる紹介、研究をした雑誌を刊行している。

［挿図2］
デネリ美術館陳列の状況

　このころから日本美術工芸をコレクションする者が現れるようになったが、そうした代表的な者がフランスのクレメンス・デネリ、ギメ、チェルヌスキー、イタリアのエドワルド・キオソーネ、ピエール・ガルーダであり、20世紀初めのスイスのアルフレッド・バウワーなどであった。キオソーネは明治政府のお雇い外国人として、日本で紙幣などの印刷技術を指導した技師であるが、彼は日本で没したため、そのコレクションはすべて日本国内滞在中に集めたものであった。彼以外は、そのほとんどはヨーロッパにおいて蒐集あるいは日本人美術商を通じて蒐集されたものであったといえる。なかでも、デネリコレクションはギメ美術館近くの邸宅の中に置かれている。その2階が陳列場となっており、階段を上がると、すぐに明、清時代の白磁、黄釉、紅釉、伊万里の色絵をはじめカラフルな色彩の獅子がアール・ヌーヴォー調の木製ケースに隙間なく置かれているのが目に飛び込んでくる。そのまわりも動物や人物が同じ種類、テーマごとにケース内に飾られている。動物、人物、楽器や家具、果物などをかたどった蒔絵の香合は小さくて、細密に表現されているが、特に、おもしろいのは根付で、60センチ四方の行灯ケース内に階段をピラミッド状に作り、四辺から積み上

げるように整然と並べられている。現在の博物館や美術館の陳列を見ている我々にとって、ちょっと異様な雰囲気というのが実感である［挿図2］。どうしてこのような状態にあるのかというと、ここはもともとデネリ夫妻の家で、自分が集め、自分が飾ったままの状態で置かれていたからである。クレメンスの遺言によって国に寄贈されたが、その条件としてケースの位置はおろか、作品もいっさい移動、置きかえることはしないという条件があったからという。つまり百年前の一人のコレクターの好尚と、楽しみ方がそのまま現在に伝わっているのである。ここでは彼女自身の日本の細密工芸に対する評価を実際に見て、感じ取ることができるのである。

　浮世絵が美術品として高く評価されたのはヨーロッパであったことはよく知られているが、印籠、根付、装剣金具といった幕末・明治の細密工芸品も、実は同じくヨーロッパのほうが早かったのである。特にこうした作品は小さく、技術も優れているため持ち帰りやすかったことも大きな理由であろう。明治時代には、外国に輸出することを目的として製作された工芸品が多く存在する。

　漆工では芝山細工と呼ばれている蒔絵や螺鈿に、象牙や金属も装飾に使用した華やかな作品。また金工では、武士や力士、町の人々を銅で鋳造して、金や銀の象嵌で装飾した「宮尾」製品、皿や塔、箪笥などを鉄板で作り、その全面に細緻な金銀の布目象嵌で唐草や有職文を表わした「駒井」製品、そして鉄や銅、銀で伊勢海老、昆虫を写実的に作り、しかもその手足を本物と同じように動かすようにした自在置物の「高瀬好山」製品。このほか京都の並河靖之の有線七宝製品など、おびただしい数の工芸品が作られていた。これらの作品は欧米では、美術館だけではなく、美術商店でもよく見かけるが、実は日本国内で探そうとすると見つけるのが困難であり、研究も外国に赴かないとできないのが現状である。

　現在、本書著者の村田理如氏をはじめ、欧米から幕末・明治期の細密工芸品を買い戻す美術愛好家が増えている。従来、幕末・明治時代の工芸の研究は、名工の作品を中心としていたが、こうした輸出目的の工芸の研究もこれからは避けて通れない分野であるといえる。

English Text

pp. 6–7

The Beauty of Late Edo and Meiji-period Crafts

Masayuki Murata
Director
Kiyomizu Sannenzaka Museum, Kyoto

I stood in front of the display case, entranced by the two inro behind the glass. I couldn't believe that such magnificent and refined beauty existed. That was twenty years ago, in a Manhattan gallery, and it marked the departure on my journey as a collector.

Most Japanese remain unaware of the crafts of the Late Edo and Meiji periods. With the majority of the finest objects in overseas collections, Japanese have few opportunities to view them, and whenever a quality piece surfaces in Japan it is immediately snapped up by foreign brokers and is sold to collectors and museums outside Japan.

The reason for the great popularity of Late Edo and Meiji-period crafts overseas is, first and foremost, their indisputable beauty, followed closely by their incredible refinement and high degree of technical accomplishment. Developing under the patronage of the samurai class, such crafts as lacquer and metalwork continued to be supported during the Meiji era by the imperial family and the system of promoting the arts and crafts instituted at that time. This continuous support contributed significantly to the outstanding achievements of Japanese artisans of the day.

During the earlier Edo period, metalwork and lacquer artisans were employed by the feudal ruling class—the shogun and daimyo—to produce sword fittings, inro, and other craft objects that were presented as gifts or part of a bride's trousseau. During the centuries of relative peace that characterized the Edo period, sword fittings evolved into magnificently decorated works of art, while inro, initially portable medicine cases, became fashion accessories decorated with the most intricate and beautiful maki-e designs.

With the Meiji Restoration of 1868, the samurai class was abolished. Lacking the patronage of the samurai, many metalwork and lacquer craftspeople suddenly found themselves unemployed and began to produce objects for commercial export to the West. At the same time, the leading masters used the superlative skills they had acquired in producing sword decorations and other decorative objects to create vases, cigarette cases, writing boxes, incense burners, and other objects for the imperial family and aristocracy, which survived the Restoration. These works were displayed at the world's fairs popular at that time, where they were garnered the highest accolades.

Eventually Western culture flooded into Japan, transforming the Japanese lifestyle and leading to a shift in Japanese art, too, toward Western ideals and values. The majority of Japanese demonstrated a stronger interest in Western culture than their own traditional arts and crafts, and the works of the great Japanese artisans faded from the national consciousness.

This is how the finest Japanese craft objects of the Late Edo and Meiji periods, once highly acclaimed both in Japan and overseas, left and continue to leave the country.

Though the great achievements of the master craftspeople of the Late Edo and Meiji periods remain in the highest estimation outside Japan even today, they go nearly completely unknown and unappreciated in their homeland. The purpose of this publication is to encourage a serious reevaluation of these craft masterpieces of the Late Edo and Meiji periods and promote and encourage their display in Japanese museums.

I would also like to express my gratitude for the writings and research of various authors in the preparation of this manuscript, too numerous to acknowledge individually.

pp. 8–15

The Collection of Kiyomizu Sannenzaka Museum

Victor Harris
Keeper Emeritus of Japanese Antiquities
The British Museum

The collections of the Kiyomizu Sannenzaka Museum consist of the finest crafts of the Edo (1600–1868) and Meiji (1868–1912) periods, which had been exported to Europe and America in the decades following the Meiji Restoration of 1868. The rapid adoption of Western material cultures into Japan at the time was paralleled by the rejection of certain aspects of Edo-period lifestyle. For example, the *haitorei* of 1876, which prohibited the wearing of swords in public, resulted in a flood of unwanted swords on the burgeoning antiques export market. The wearing of Western clothes made certain accessories largely obsolete. These included inro, the decorative containers for personal seals or medicine which were carried suspended by cords from the sash, and netsuke, the ornamental toggles which fixed the cords at the belt. Changes in communication, particularly in printing and illustration, signaled an end to the traditional woodblock processes. Pen and ink gradually ousted the brush and ink stone and the traditional lacquered writing boxes. Thus swords, decorative metal sword fittings, inro, netsuke, and fine lacquered writing boxes all became available to Western collectors for the first time.

Whereas Japan had been at peace with her neighbors throughout the Edo period, the nations of Europe had been more or less at constant war with each other and involved in campaigns of imperial expansion in India, Asia, Africa, and elsewhere. Consequently large numbers of weapons, including swords of diverse cultures, had been in free circulation. In comparison with the swords of all other nations, the superiority of the Japanese sword, both as a weapon and as an art object, was immediately evident. Not only was the Japanese sword functionally superior to those of all nations and cultures, but the elegance and quality of its lacquered scabbard and the fine decorative metal hilt fittings were immediately appealing.

Japanese lacquer-ware itself had been known in the West since the seventeenth century in the form of lacquered chests, tables, shelves, and similar furniture exported from Nagasaki by the Dutch East Indies Company. Just as porcelain was known in Europe as "China," so lacquer was known as "Japan." European attempts to duplicate lacquer, such as "shellac," were devised, but they could not match the quality of the true Japanese ware. Although much of the Edo-period export lacquer was of fine quality, for the most part it did not compare with the writing boxes, incense boxes, small chests of drawers, and inro which had been made for the samurai, aristocrat, and wealthy merchant classes in Japan at the time. These things were simply far superior in quality to anything seen in Europe before the Meiji Restoration, even though the Shogunate, Japan's military government of the day, had facilitated the export of lacquer shortly after the port of Yokohama was opened to trade in 1859.

The British diplomat Rutherford Alcock had displayed a large collection of Japanese material at the second International Exposition in 1862, mainly consisting of everyday objects. But the hundred or so pieces sent from Japan to the 1867 Paris Exposition by a delegation under the leadership of the fourteen-year-old Tokugawa Akitake were of altogether higher quality. They consisted of arms, amour, ceramics, textiles, lacquer, and luxury objects which had been in everyday use during the Edo period.

In the first decades of the Meiji era, the traditional crafts was an area in which Japan saw itself as competing with other nations on an industrial scale, and Japanese objects were highly acclaimed at succeeding international expositions. There was Vienna in 1873, followed by Philadelphia in 1876, Amsterdam in 1883, Antwerp in 1885, Barcelona in 1888, Chicago in 1893, Paris in 1900, and by Saint Louis in 1904.

The Meiji-period craftsmen naturally turned their hand to ornamental work for export. Overseas collectors avidly bought their work. For example in London the Victoria and Albert Museum bought a collection of "Nagasaki" lacquer in 1852 from the London art dealer Hewitts & Co, many ceramics which had been exhibited at the Philadelphia exhibition in 1876, and thereafter many pieces from various expositions and dealers, including the huge bronze decorative incense burner by Suzuki Chokichi, which had appeared in the Paris exposition, for the immense sum of 1,500 pounds. The museum had been founded in order to "exhibit the practical application of the principles of design in the graceful arrangement of forms and the harmonious combination of colors for the benefit of manufacturers, artisans, and the general public." It was precisely in these areas that the Japanese craftsmen excelled. The traditional designs were new and exciting, and the hybrid designs based on feedback from the West were applied to export ware by the Japanese craftsmen using their traditional skills to great effect.

Although the museums collected with enthusiasm, the very best of the Meiji-period wares were bought by rich and discerning collectors. Since the objects were made for export, very few remained in Japan, except for a number bought personally by the Emperor and the Imperial Household Agency. Today there are some collections in a small number of specialist museums like the National Museum of Modern Art and a certain amount of material in Tokyo National Museum and other larger museums. But a growing awareness of the importance of the art of the late nineteenth and early twentieth centuries has resulted in a small number of Japanese collectors traveling overseas to recover this lost heritage. Mr. Murata, the director of the Kiyomizu Sannenzaka Museum, has built up over the years the most significant collection of high-quality pieces to be found anywhere in the world, including the traditional and export metalwork of the sword-fittings makers, the lacquer artists, the decorative enameled ceramic ware of the "Satsuma" type, and the unique Meiji era cloisonné of the top makers.

Both late Edo-period and Meiji-era sword fittings by the greatest makers, such as Goto Ichijo and Kano Natsuo, are complemented by ornamental pieces that the Sannenzaka Museum has recovered from Europe and America. The silver-cased pocket watch with a carved and inlaid peony (plate 172) by Kano Natsuo has a distinctive flavor that emphasizes the contrast between the Western object and the Japanese decoration. A short sword blade by the Oei-era (1394–1428) smith Genzaemon Nobukuni is mounted with gold fittings and a scabbard of carved black lacquer (plates 125–27) by Shoami Katsuyoshi, probably among the best if not the best set of sword fittings by that artist. The mounting must have been commissioned by a daimyo or other high-ranking samurai, and would probably never left Japan. It contrasts with a silver ornamental incense burner decorated with cockerels and hens (plates 166–167) in high-relief colored metal inlays made by Katsuyoshi after the *haitorei*.

Part of the charm of the traditional Japanese metalwork was the range of colored alloys and manufacturing techniques which were new to the West. The method of engraving called *katagiribori*, in which the chisel is used at varying angles and depths to create lines simulating ink brush strokes on paper, showed how metal sculpture could be the equivalent of painting. The elegance of deliberately rusted iron, the black alloy *shakudo*, and the silver-grey-brown range of colors of the alloy *shibuichi*, (three parts copper to one part silver), and the use of varied silver, gold, and other colored metal inlays brought a new dimension to the decorative arts.

Such metalwork naturally commanded very high prices, but there was a great division in distribution of wealth in the West in those days, and the wealthy had a respect for the arts and crafts. People regarded the objects offered at the expositions with much the same degree of enthusiasm as people regard the efforts of today's Olympic athletes, and Japan was constantly winning prizes at the international expositions

The highest quality lacquer wares were compared with European shellac, Chinese lacquer, and Edo-period export work, and were found to be far superior in all respects. Like the metalwork, lacquer was the vehicle for high art, a mixture of painting and sculpture in an exotic and exciting medium. Gold maki-e—made by settling gold dust into the lacquer coating on objects—in particular excited attention with its appearance resembling solid gold. Europeans must have recalled the words of Marco Polo, who had spoken of the land of "Zipangu," where the buildings were clad with gold. There were also several uniquely Japanese techniques of using small amounts of gold to give radiant effects. There was no Western equivalent—for example, of the technique of *nashiji*, in which gold or other particles set beneath the surface of translucent lacquer sparkled like stars on a clear night. Edo-period inro, which appeared in the West for the first time during the Meiji era, exhibited all the techniques of the lacquer artist, and, like the metal craftsmen of the late Edo period the lacquerers made larger objects for presentation at the world fairs.

Some objects were utilitarian, such as traditional boxes in which jewelry and such treasures could be kept, and some were purely ornamental, such as the extraordinary pair of plaques (plates 197–98) by Shirayama Shosai illustrating a heron beneath the sun and a crow beneath the moon. The plaques had all the ingredients of a major work of art in the technical excellence of the lacquer work itself, the haunting beauty of the composition, and the very "Japaneseness" of the subject matter. Nothing made today either in Japan or elsewhere can match the quality and exuberance of such works.

Together with inro came the exquisite netsuke. These miniature sculptures brought the Edo-period culture fresh and vivid to foreign shores at the beginning of the Meiji period, just as they transport us back to the Edo period today. The Sannenzaka collection has a unique selection of inro in fine condition with their original netsuke still attached.

The enlightened Meiji Emperor was fully aware of the place the arts and crafts of Japan had to play in the world. The Emperor had become well known and loved in Europe and the United States, as he was in Japan, and the Imperial Family was effective in bringing the Japanese culture to the attention of the international community. The Emperor personally supported the craftsmen by buying their exhibits in the domestic exhibitions. At the Third Japan Domestic Industrial Exhibition of 1890 the most expensive objects were bought by the Imperial Household and a small number of rich foreign collectors. Before that at the Japan Art Association in Kyoto the Emperor had personally bought thirty-two objects, the Empress Mother eighteen, and the Imperial Household Agency twenty-seven pieces. The Emperor gave the huge sum of 20,000 yen in support of the next exhibition. In addition, the Imperial Household Agency commissioned gifts for foreign dignitaries and royalty marked with the Imperial Chrysanthemum crest. These include pairs of silver vases, cloisonné vases, and lacquer boxes. Sometimes swords were commissioned, like the long sword made by Sugawara Kanenori as a gift for Britain's first full ambassador in Japan, Sir Claude MacDonald, and which is now in the collection of the Victoria and Albert Museum in London. Four generations or so have passed since that time, and such treasured heirlooms must of necessity come onto the market as family fortunes fail. The Kiyomizu Sannenzaka Museum has acquired a number of such significant historical masterpieces, which must have once graced the dressers of stately European homes, and which are now to be seen by the Japanese public for the first time.

Fine enameled ceramics made by potters in Kyoto and elsewhere, named after their place of origin in Satsuma, and the unique Japanese cloisonné ware, are further distinct areas in which The Kiyomizu Sannenzaka Museum specializes. The lord of Satsuma Province had sent a delegation to the Paris Exposition of 1867, where the gold and colored enamel ceramic ware was greatly admired. Following the further successes by Satsuma Province, the style of pottery body and decoration was taken up by artists like Kinkozan, Yabu Meizan, both of Kyoto, and others. The best Satsuma decoration is found on smaller pieces of ceramic, lavishly enameled with the ubiquitous gold, and painted minutely in vivid colors—work of a quality inconceivable to Western potters. But the cloisonné was possibly the most impressive of all the crafts to Western eyes. The tradition of enameling on metal is of great antiquity in Europe, and there were skilled French makers of *champleve*. Chinese cloisonné was also well known, but lacked the delicacy and freshness of the Japanese work. The delicacy of the wirework and the freshness of the colors of the best of cloisonné, such as the work of Namikawa Sosuke and Namikawa Yasuyuki—both appointed as Artist to the Imperial Household—was, again, beyond the capability of any Western artist. It may be no exaggeration to say that the Kiyomizu Sannenzaka Museum represents the flowering of Japanese craftsmanship which will never be equaled.

pp. 18–20

Kyoto Cloisonné of Namikawa Yasuyuki

I first encountered the cloisonné of Namikawa Yasuyuki (1845–1927) more than a decade ago in a London gallery. I will never forget my powerful emotional reaction upon examining it closely. Against a black background, intense reds, greens, and blues stood out brightly within outlines of beautiful gold and silver, depicting a lovely and magical design of birds and flowers. I was even more astonished when I learned it had been created over a century ago. The form was sleekly contemporary and the design extremely sophisticated and timeless.

I was unfamiliar with the name Namikawa Yasuyuki at the time, as no doubt many still are today. But visitors to the Kiyomozu Sannenzaka Museum in Kyoto of which I am director, when seeing the cloisonné masterpieces of Namikawa and other Meiji-period masters, are always astonished that this beautiful art once flourished in Japan.

Japanese cloisonné dates back to before the Nara period (710–94), but it became widespread from the mid-1800s, the late Edo period. Prior to then, several cloisonné techniques were used for detailing such objects as decorative nail covers and sword guards, but it was not a particularly popular craft.

Late Edo and Meiji cloisonné traces its roots back to Kaji Tsunekichi (1808–83) of Nagoya, who purchased a cloisonné piece—probably of Chinese manufacture—from a Dutch merchant, analyzed it, and discovered and applied the techniques of cloisonné with wires. The craft was transmitted to Kyoto from the 1870s, where Namikawa Yasuyuki focused on cloisonné with wires as the epitome of the craft in Japan and elevated it to an art.

Cloisonné with wires is produced by drawing the design on the body of the piece, then attaching flattened wires of gold, silver, and brass in the shape of the design to the body with a glue derived from orchids. Silver solder is then applied and the piece is fired to firmly attach the wires to the body. Next cloisonné enamels are applied with a brush inside the wire outlines (known as cells) and the piece is again fired. This process is repeated six to seven times until the wire outlines are covered over. At this stage the piece is polished with successively finer scouring powders. The enormous amount of labor and skill required to complete a single piece contributed to the early demise of the art.

Namikawa Yasuyuki was born in Kyoto, the third son of the Takaoka family, bailiffs of the Omi domain in Kawagoe. When he was eleven years old, the head of the related Namikawa family suddenly died, and the boy was adopted into the family. The Namikawas were imperial retainers but also produced cloisonné as a sideline. Yasuyuki began to work in cloisonné in 1873 and showed his first work at the Kyoto Exhibition in 1875.

The sophistication, grace, refinement, beautiful colors, and bold compositions of Namikawa's work won the admiration of Westerners. He was honored with prizes at the Philadelphia World's Fair in 1876 and the Paris World's Fair in 1878, and he won a gold medal at the 1889 Paris World's Fair. He also won prizes at the First Japanese National Exposition to Promote Industry in 1877 as well as a special prize for achievement at the same show in 1890. All in all, he was awarded thirty-one prizes and awards for his work at various exhibitions both abroad and in Japan, including eleven gold prizes, seven silver prizes, and four bronze prizes.

The majority of his work was purchased by wealthy non-Japanese individuals or foreign museums, and even a small piece 10 centimeters in height sold for the equivalent at that time of a secretary's annual earnings. Such prices placed him far beyond the reach of Japanese collectors.

In 1896, Namikawa was designated an artist under the patronage of the imperial household (*teishitsu gigei in*) and his pieces were purchased by the Imperial Household Agency and presented to important foreign guests. The only place in Japan his works could be found were his own workshop, and the majority of the few pieces that turn up in Japan were gifts presented by Emperor Meiji to Japanese subjects.

A few of Namikawa Yasuyuki's works are over thirty centimeters in height, but most are quite small, ranging from five to twenty centimeters. Many relatively small things are renowned for their great beauty—for example, gemstones, netsuke, Persian miniatures, and Paul Klee's paintings—and Namikawa Yasuyuki's work belongs to this group of tiny treasures.

pp. 34–50

Owari Cloisonné and Works by Namikawa Sosuke

pp. 34–36

Owari Cloisonné

Cloisonné with wires emerged in Owari Province (modern Aichi Prefecture) in the mid-1800s but remained technically undeveloped until the 1870s. Unlike other crafts such as ceramics, maki-e, and metalwork with their long histories and traditions, cloisonné with wires was a relatively new craft in Japan.

At the beginning, an opaque enamel similar to that used in Chinese cloisonné—called *doro shippo*, or "paste enamels"—was used in Japan. When a cell (the area enclosed by wire to depict the image) was too large, however, cracks tended to appear in the enamel during firing, so it was necessary to include numerous additional support wires unrelated to the outline of the design, merely to hold the enamel in place. Both of these elements limited freedom of artistic expression in cloisonné.

In a relatively short period of time, however—especially when compared to maki-e and metalwork, with their centuries of tradition—cloisonné exhibited remarkable development. The German scientist Gottfried Wagner played a pivotal role. Visiting Japan in 1868, Wagner introduced the most advanced molding and firing techniques to Japanese ceramic craftsman in Arita (Saga Prefecture) and various other regions.

At the same time, new glazes and enamels were being developed in Nagoya and Kyoto, for both ceramics and cloisonné. Cloisonné techniques made giant strides and it was now possible to fire enamel to large areas of the body without additional support wires. Furthermore, bright new colors and transparent enamels were developed, and by 1877 Japanese cloisonné emerged as a major export product.

The major cloisonné-producing region at the time was Tojima Village in Kaito-gun (modern Shippo-cho, Ama-gun, Aichi Prefecture), represented by the cloisonné master Hayashi Kodenji (1831–1915). Hayashi Kodenji had studied cloisonné with Hayashi Shogoro, the direct disciple of Kaji Tsunekichi, and he opened his own workshop in 1863, quickly producing high-quality pieces for export. He also worked to develop glazes and to improve production techniques. Hayashi built a gallery to display his work in Tojima Village, established a school to teach cloisonné techniques, and made a major contribution to modern Japanese cloisonné. At the time brass was most widely used for the wire frames of cloisonné, but Hayashi introduced the frequent use of gold and silver wires, imparting a luxurious touch to his pieces. Other Owari cloisonné masters whose work enjoys a high reputation overseas are Kumeno Teitaro (1863–1939), Kawade Shibataro (b. 1856), Hattori Tadasaburo, and Ando Jubei.

Kumeno is known for the fineness of his outlines, and he produced many remarkable masterpieces. Kawade was the head of the Ando Cloissoné Workshop, which continues production to this day. Very few of his works survive, but each is on a different subject and they are extremely well crafted. Hattori and Ando, together with Kawade, continued to lead the advance in cloisonné techniques. They are thought to be the first to employ the technique of relief cloisonné, in which areas of the design are built up higher than the rest of the surface. They also engraved sections of the body with a design and then covered it with transparent enamel.

While Japanese cloisonné was the best in the world at the time, there was one technique in which the French excelled: *pique-a-jour*, in which portions of the base were dissolved with nitric acid, leaving only the enamel and the wire outlines. Kawade Shibataro and Ando Jubei were quick to introduce this technique to Japan.

As we have seen, craftsmen from Owari were at the technological forefront of Japanese cloisonné. But Kyoto cloisonné made little use of these new techniques. There, the traditional methods of wire cloisonné so ably employed by Namikawa Yasuyuki continued to be used and developed. Cloisonné manufacture advanced along different paths in Owari and Kyoto.

p. 50
Works by Namikawa Sosuke

One of the greatest cloisonné masters of the Meiji era (1868–1912) was Namikawa Sosuke (1847–1910) of Tokyo, who created the thirty-two cloisonné panels that decorate the dining rooms of the former Akasaka Detached Palace, now known as the Official Guest House. Born in Hebizono, Tsurumaki, Shimosa Province (modern Asahi-shi, Chiba Prefecture), Sosuke perfected the technique of cloisonné without wires in 1879. The process is the same as cloisonné with wires, but the wires—either in their entirety or in certain portions of the design—are removed before the final firing. A soft, blended edge is created when the wires are removed, reproducing the subtle shading that is a distinctive feature of Japanese painting.

Namikawa Sosuke began as a ceramics merchant, but he was so bewitched by the cloisonné pieces he saw at the 1877 first Japanese National Exposition to Promote Industry that he decided to learn the craft. He purchased the cloisonné factory of the German Ahrens company located in Kameido and trained the Owari cloisonné craftsmen working there until the technique of wireless cloisonné was perfected. In 1887 he also acquired the Tokyo Branch Workshop of the Dainippon Shippo Seizo Kaisha based in Nagoya. Given these facts, it is clear that Namikawa Sosuke's cloisonné was most closely linked to the Owari lineage.

His aim was to recreate Japanese painting in the medium of cloisonné, yet the pieces he created were not mere copies of paintings but exhibited a unique depth and vibrancy that can only be realized in cloisonné.

His achievements led to him being selected, along with Kyoto cloisonné-with-wires master Namikawa Yasuyuki, as an artist under the patronage of the imperial household (*teishitsu gigei in*) in 1896. They were the only two cloisonné artists to be so honored.

Namikawa Sosuke continued to pursue the aesthetics of Japanese painting in the cloisonné medium, specializing in cloisonné without wires, throughout his career. While other cloisonné artists began to employ Sosuke's techniques, Namikawa Yasuyuki of Kyoto remained dedicated to the cloisonné with wires method to the end, believing that the gold and silver outlines of the wires were an important element in the unique beauty of cloisonné. As such, the two masters embodied two unique approaches to their art.

pp. 56–58

Kyoto Satsuma Ware

The miniature is an important category in the arts —the best-known genre of this type being perhaps Persian and Mughal miniatures. Delight and wonder at small and highly detailed works is universal, —when, of course, miniaturization increases and intensifies an object's beauty. The viewer is astonished by the precision of technique and perseverance required to create such works, and the artist feels a well-deserved pride in his unrivaled skill at being able to create something so perfect on such a tiny scale. Such are the joys of miniatures.

Miniature paintings of the sort found in Persia and India did not develop in Japan; rather, a focus on miniaturization was seen in other genres such as cloisonné and metalwork. The closest equivalent to the tiny, highly detailed scenes of Persian miniatures may perhaps be the painting on Kyoto Satsuma ware.

Satsuma ware was first produced during the Momoyama period (1568–1600) in Satsuma and Osumi (modern Kagoshima Prefecture) by ceramic artisans from the Korean Peninsula. In the late Edo period, ceramics with highly detailed painted decoration in gold and colors were being fired at the Naeshirogawa kiln.

At the first Paris World's Fair in which Japan participated, held in 1867, Satsuma Province independently exhibited Satsuma ware, which was very well received. At the 1873 Vienna World's Fair, the twelfth-generation head of the Chin family, Chin Jukan (1835–1906), exhibited a large vase that also won accolades. These two world fairs firmly established the praiseworthy reputation of Satsuma ware overseas. Following this, Satsuma-style painted pottery enjoyed a boom in major Japanese cities such as Kyoto, Osaka, Nagoya, Tokyo, and Yokohama. The majority of the wares were exported, creating international recognition of "Satsuma" as a distinct type of Japanese ceramics. As Japan did not manufacture industrial goods at the time, Satsuma ware, together with other ceramics and cloisonné, was an important export. Satsuma ware produced by the Kinkozan workshop in Kyoto and the Osaka Yabu Meizan Satsuma ware were in especially high demand overseas as rival "brands."

The Kinkozan family was a well-known producer of Awata ware from the mid-Edo period. The sixth-generation head of the family, Kinkozan Sobei (d. 1884), was very sensitive to the trends of his day and from 1872 began to incorporate elements of Satsuma-ware style into his productions, creating what later came to be known as Kyoto Satsuma ware.

The seventh-generation Kinkozan Sobei (1868–1927), taking over at the death of his father, followed in his predecessor's footsteps by producing designs of highly detailed and graceful birds-and-flowers compositions. His work won a silver medal at the 1889 Paris World's Fair, when he was only 21. At the time the Kinkozan workshop located at Awataguchi was the largest in the area, with over 200 artisans.

Numerous other kilns in the Awataguchi area of Higashiyama were producing Satsuma ware. In addition to Yabu Meizan and Kinkozan, we find many other art signatures, including Seikozan, Hankinzan, Shizan, Meizan, Kaizan, Sessan, and Kozan, but very little research had been done on which were produced in Kyoto and which were from other locales; generally, only Kinkozan-style painted ware is known as Kyoto Satsuma.

Yabu Meizan (1853–1934) was born in Osaka as the second son of the painter Yabu Chosui. He studied painting in Tokyo, then returned to Osaka where in 1880 he opened a Satsuma-style painted pottery workshop in Nakanoshima, where he produced unique works characterized by highly detailed landscapes and decorative motifs that received numerous prizes at exhibitions and fairs both in and outside Japan. Yabu earned an extremely high reputation overseas for his consistently fine, highly decorative and detailed works.

The 1893 Chicago World's Fair proved to be a major turning point for Satsuma ware, as the first sign of a wane in its popularity became apparent. At the fin d'siecle, people desired novelty, and new trends in art such as Art Nouveau were beginning to have an impact on taste.

The fine works exhibited by Kinkozan at the fair were poorly received, and Kinkozan Sobei reacted by adopting new designs, styles, and techniques and creating pieces in an Art Nouveau style. Yabu Meizan, on the other hand, chose to forgo innovation in favor of striving to perfect the traditional style he had developed.

In spite of their poor reception at the Chicago World's Fair, the work of both workshops continued to sell well, and though the kilns are no longer in existence there are many avid collectors of both wares around the world.

pp. 68–70

Inro

Inro are small cases for carrying medicines that were originally used when traveling. The word inro originally referred to a case (*ro*) for a personal seal (*in*). By the early Edo period, it had come to be used for carrying medicine, though the old name persisted. With the new function came the practice of decorating the surface of the case.

Inro were used by travelers of all classes. Generally they had three or four compartments, each for a different kind of medicine. Inro were hung from the kimono sash, or obi, and were part of a set: the inro; a netsuke, attached to the end of the inro's silk cord that was tucked into the obi; and the ojime, a bead on silk threads used to secure the lid of the inro. Some inro were not carried hung from the obi but tucked into the breast of the kimono instead.

Most inro are made of either several layers of Japanese paper stiffened with glue and lacquer, or of wood, but there are also inro of metal, cloisonné, ceramics, and ivory.

As the Edo period neared its end, inro became increasingly decorative, evolving from their original function as a travel accessory into a fashion ornament. People owned several and wore different ones for different occasions—somewhat like a necktie or a bag today, though much more luxurious.

Fine inro are decorated with maki-e, inlaid with engraved gold, silver, or copper alloy design elements, and decorated with such costly materials as ivory, tortoiseshell, and coral.

The shogun and feudal lords (daimyo) employed maki-e artisans who created the inro they wore. By the last decades of the Edo period, members of the merchant class had far surpassed the samurai in wealth, and they commissioned maki-e artisans to produce luxurious inro for them. The craftsman lavished their highly developed skills on these small masterpieces, often inventing new techniques to create beautiful inro. Partly as a result, maki-e and metalwork reached an apogee in Japanese history from the mid- to late-Edo periods.

When foreigners began to visit Japan after the 1868 Meiji Restoration and opening of the nation, they were enraptured by the beauty of inro, and they purchased many fine pieces. Major non-Japanese collectors accumulated hundreds or even a thousand inro—such figures as the English industrialist Michael Tomkinson (1841–1921); the Swiss Maurice C. Champoud (d. 1981), managing director of the giant food company Nestle in Kobe, Japan; the Dutchman Willem Pieter Groeneveldt (1841–1915); Alfred Baur (1865–1951) of Switzerland; Italian Ugo Alfonso Casal (1888–1968); and American attorney Raymond Bushell (1910–98). These renowned international collectors—among many others—have assembled many first-rate works.

Unfortunately, the only Japanese inro collector of note is Baron Takei Morimasa (1842–1926)—a sad state of affairs considering this is their land of origin. Whenever a high-quality inro comes up for sale in Japan, it is immediately purchased by a foreign dealer. Japanese collectors eagerly invest huge sums in Japanese modern art and Western Impressionist paintings, but are unwilling to do likewise for the art works of the Late Edo and Meiji periods. During the Meiji period, a fine inro cost about the same as the average home. Even today, a high-quality inro can normally be purchased for about two million yen. It would be wonderful if Japanese collectors would take a serious interest in this magnificent product of their own culture and build significant collections here.

pp. 80–82

Netsuke

Perhaps no other object of Japanese material culture has ever disappeared as quickly and as completely as the netsuke. Just a generation or two ago, you could find one in every household. A little digging and one or two were certain to turn up in any older home. My own grandfather had a netsuke that he kept with his old coins.

Together with kimono, netsuke were a central part of Japanese culture. Unlike Western clothes, kimono lack pockets. Any object that couldn't be easily tucked into the sleeves or the breast had to be hung from the obi. A variety of small objects fell under the heading of *sagemono* (hanging things), among them flint bags (for flints used to start a fire when traveling), purses, tobacco containers, and inro.

Originally such *sagemono* were tied together with a cord and draped over the obi, some hanging in front of the obi and others hanging behind, held in place by the obi. In the early Edo period a metal ring was passed over the obi and the *sagemono* tied to it. Soon the metal ring was no longer looped through the obi but instead tucked up underneath it and allowed to fall over the obi in front, with the cord holding the *sagemono* held between the obi and the kimono. Netsuke evolved from this metal ring.

Netsuke come in innumerable shapes, but they are categorized generally into *kagamibuta* (mirror-lid), *manju* (bun), *ryusa* (openwork), *hakogata* (box), *sashi* (inserted), and *katabori* (carved figure).

Kagamibuta netsuke are round, flattened shapes made of ivory or wood with an inset metal disk. *Manju* netsuke are in the flattened oval shape of a Japanese bean-jam bun. *Ryusa* netsuke are similar in shape to *manju* netsuke, but are hollow and carved in openwork, depicting people or animals. Box netsuke are box-shaped with a lid, many of them lacquered and decorated with maki-e. Inserted netsuke are elongated in form, for inserting into the obi. *Katabori* netsuke are carved completely in three dimensions, detailing each part of the figure or subject, often a plant, animal, or person.

Netsuke depict innumerable subjects, from animals, plants, and insects to people, deities, imaginary creatures, tools and implements, folk tales and legends, Buddhist figures, Noh masks, and ghosts and monsters. They are made from a wide variety of materials. Though wood and ivory are most common, they may also be carved from animal teeth, bone, horses hooves, bamboo, wisteria, or fashioned from lacquer, metal, ceramic, nuts, glass, stone, coral, or abalone shell.

Netsuke are also shaped by numerous functional requirements. They cannot snag the kimono or project in such a way as to cause discomfort to the wearer. They need to be carefully weighted so that the front faces outward, and the eye through which the cord is passed must be conveniently located. One of the charms of netsuke is the way carvers accommodate these requirements while still creating delightful pieces.

Netsuke carvers made free use of materials and themes to create vibrant and lively works. While inro were originally an accessory of the warrior class, netsuke developed from the beginning under the patronage of townspeople. As a result, while inro production was centered in the power centers of Tokyo and Kyoto, distinctive netsuke were also created in various regional cities as Gifu, Nara, and Shimane. Many of these regional netsuke are humorous, comical pieces—a trait very rarely exhibited by inro.

Like inro, however, netsuke began pouring out of Japan from the late Edo and Meiji periods. Their convenient size and ingenious designs attracted foreign appreciators, and large numbers were purchased as gifts and collectibles. As was the case with ukiyo-e, netsuke were so familiar a part of daily life that Japanese failed to recognize their artistic worth.

Baron Go Seinosuke (1865–1942) was one of the first Japanes to take note of this. A major entrepreneur of his day—member of the House of Peers, director of the Tokyo Stock Exchange, and chairman of the Tokyo Chamber of Commerce and Industry—he was also an avid collector of netsuke, systematically assembling famous pieces by major carvers and warning the Japanese people that they were in danger of losing important cultural artifacts. After his death, his collection of 272 netsuke was donated to the Imperial Museum, today's Tokyo National Museum.

Many museums and private collectors have collections of over one thousand netsuke, among them the British Museum and The Metropolitan Museum in New York. Most of the research on netsuke has also been in the West and is published in Western languages. Unfortunately, Baron Go's worst fears seem to have materialzed.

pp. 88–90

Sword Fittings

Relatively few swords, sword guards, and other sword fittings have made their way into foreign collections, and those that have were acquired later than netsuke, inro, and other types of crafts. One reason was that the samurai traditionally valued their swords as highly as their lives, and no matter how dire their economic straits were reluctant to part with them. Furthermore, Japanese in general still have a great appreciation for swords, and there are many domestic collectors.

The metalworking techniques used in sword and sword fitting production can be roughly divided into three types: casting, hammering, and decorative chasing. Up through the Heian period, Japanese metalworking focused on creating Buddhist images and ritual appurtenances. From the Kamakura period on, when the nation's rule passed to the warrior class, military equipment such as armor, swords, and sword fittings came to dominate the art. Japan is unique in that in most other cultures metalwork developed primarily around the production of personal ornaments.

The history of Japanese swordmaking can be traced back to copper swords and lances produced during the Yayoi era (300 BCE–AD 300). By the fifth century, the Kofun or Tumulus period, iron swords were being made, and some show evidence of decorative openwork, engraving, and chasing. The decorative impulse intensifies in the Nara period, and the first long swords (*tachi*), known as *kurozukuri*, are produced. The sheaths are of black lacquer, and the fittings are simply designed ironwork. They are distinguished by their functionality and lack of decoration.

In the subsequent Heian period, the large *tachi* swords of warriors were decorated with maki-e and mother-of-pearl, and fittings were engraved with birds-and-flowers and Chinese arabesque (*karakusa*) designs—indicating that the warrior class was beginning to take an interest in applying decorative touches to their weaponry.

As the warriors adopted the practice of wearing a short sword (*koshigatana*) at all times, even indoors, greater attention was paid to their decoration. The fittings that accompanied the short sword were the sword pommel or buttcap (*kashira*), hilt ornaments (*menuki*), hilt cover (*tsutsugane*), hilt collar (*fuchi*), and scabbard end (*kojiri*); at times they also included a hairpick (*kogai*) and accessory knife (*kozuka*). Attached to the side of the sword, the *kogai* was used to scratch the head or the ears. Women used a similar accessory, often fashioned of tortoiseshell, which they inserted in their hair. Technically, the *kozuka* is the name of the hilt of the small accessory knife (*kogatana*) attached to the side of the sword and used to cut cord or paper.

When the *tachi* was superseded by the curved *uchigatana*-style sword in the latter half of the Muromachi period, these same accessories were retained and further developed and adorned, exhibiting tremendous evolution.

The first major change in sword fittings occurred in the mid-Muromachi period, when Goto Yujo, the founder of the Goto clan decorated a base of *shakudo*—an alloy of copper and gold, with a maximum of eight-percent gold—with a hammered *nanako* (fish-roe) pattern and applied relief designs of dragons and lions. This new treatment, like the lacquer technique of building up gold relief designs on a black lacquer ground, imparted a new luxury and refinement to swords. The Goto family continued to supply swords and fittings to Japan's military rulers for seventeen generations, including the Ashikagas, the Toyotomis, and the Tokugawas, until the end of the Edo period. This style was known as *iebori* and was considered the epitome of formal style in the Edo period.

The next major change was in the use of colored metals, and took place in the Momoyama period. Umetada Myoju of Nishijin in Kyoto created sword guards with pictorial designs using gold, silver, copper, brass, and *shakudo* in a skillful flat-inlay technique. At the time, the sword guards of most *uchigatana* were made of iron, and sword guards of colored metal were a dramatic innovation.

With the arrival of the Edo period, there were no more major military activities, and a long age of relative peace began. During this time, sword fittings grew increasingly decorative and aesthetically pleasing.

From the mid-Edo period in particular, the "three great metalworkers of Nara"—Tsuchiya Yasuchika, Sugiura Joi, and Nara Toshinaga—were active, as well as Yokoya Somin, the founder of the popular style of metal decoration (*machibori*, in contrast to the above-mentioned *iebori*). Developing such new techniques as *shishiaibori* (low relief carving), *katagiribori* (chiseling), and *suemon* (raised inlay), and employing a wide variety of metals that included gold, silver, *shakudo*, copper, brass, and *shibuichi* (an alloy of copper and silver), they created many distinctive and vibrantly colorful pieces. Their more flamboyant approach took shape as the *machibori* style.

Japanese metalworkers used numerous techniques and a wide variety of metals to create richly expressive works of an incomparable degree of beauty and sophistication, but after the Meiji period the craft has declined inexorably.

---

pp. 102–104, 108–110

Metalwork

The new Meiji government was born in 1868, after 250 years of feudal Tokugawa reign. Metalwork was the craft most affected by this change. The metalworkers who had been employed by the shogun and the rest of the military ruling class in producing swords and their fittings suddenly found themselves without work. This was compounded by the government's 1876 order banning the wearing of swords, the *haitorei*.

There was a limited demand for sword guards as art objects, but it was not sufficient to sustain a livelihood, and metalworkers were forced to explore other means to make use of their highly developed skills. They found it in the production of metal kimono accessories and tobacco containers, as well as decorative objects, vases, plates, incense burners, and cigarette cases for export.

The Japanese government also sought to promote domestic industry. Japan, which had been closed to the outside world for centuries, had no manufacturing industries to speak of, and its only potential exports were its craft products. The government focused in particular on the unemployed metalwork artisans.

At the time, the majority of metal objects produced in the West were bronze or silver castings. The intricately engraved and inlaid products of many different metals—gold, silver, copper, *shakudo*, *shibuichi*, and so forth—produced in Japan were a great novelty. The Japanese government not only exhibited but also sold these objects at the many world's fairs and international exhibitions of the day, and thus succeeded in creating a powerful demand for them.

In order to encourage the continuity and development of such crafts, in 1890 the government established the system of artisans designated as enjoying the patronage of the imperial household. This designation meant that the artist or artisan received substantial orders from the imperial family and the Imperial Household Agency, achieving a level of economic security and social recognition. At about the same time the Tokyo School of the Arts opened, and Kano Natsuo (1828–98), the first metalworker to be designated an artist under the patronage of the imperial household, became the first instructor of metalworking there, transmitting his skills to many successors. This was a great source of encouragement to his fellow artists.

In subsequent years such leading Meiji-period masters of metalwork as Unno Shomin (1844–1915), Kagawa Katsuhiro (1853–1917), and Tsukada Shukyo (1848–1918) were designated artists under the patronage of the imperial household. Though not so designated, Shoami Katsuyoshi (1832–1908) was also a highly accomplished metalwoker.

The Meiji era was a turbulent time for metalworkers, but though they faced such daunting challenges as the collapse of the warrior class and the opening of Japan to the world, they were able to employ their highly developed skills in fashioning sword fittings to produce incomparable art objects in metal with great pictorial skill, and they deserve high praises for their efforts and abilities.

The metalworkers designated as under the patronage of the imperial household continued to win numerous awards at international exhibitions. Their work was purchased by foreign collectors and museums, as well as commissioned by the Imperial Household Agency as gifts for important foreign visitors. At the same time, many sword fittings made by anonymous artisans were exported by brokers (*shokuhinka*) and found their way foreign collections.

Brokers made their debut when Japan took part in its first world's fair, the Vienna World's Fair of 1873. Brokers were individuals or companies that commissioned works from artisans and then exhibited them in shows or exported them under their owen brand name. Some of the more active brokers of the period were the Kiryu Kosho Kaisha, the Kanazawa Doki Kaisha, and the individual Ozeki Yahei. Some of these firms had shops in Yokohama where they sold directly to foreigners. A few also had overseas branches.

The Kiryu Kosho Kaisha commissioned works from the leading craftspeople but presented the artisans with designs for the decoration and forms of the pieces they ordered. The company went out of business in 1891. Perhaps because it was a semi-governmental organization, it lacked a solid grasp of the market and was the first of the brokerage firms to close its doors. They tried to sell their inventory in New York and Paris at the time, but were unable to do so because it was already quite outdated.

The Kanazawa Doki Kaisha was established in 1877 in Naga-machi, Kanazawa-ku, Ishikawa-ken with the aim of assisting metalworkers and exporting new products overseas. Among those involved in the company's founding were leading Kanazawa artisans such as Mizuno Genroku Mitsuharu (1838–95) and Yamakawa Koji (1828–82).

Ozeki Yahei was especially wellknown in the West as a broker for the highest quality metalwork objects. Ozeki commissioned works from such leading metalworkers as Unno Moritoshi, Yamada Motonobu, Kaneyasu Masatoshi, and Ikeda Minkoku—all of which appeared in exhibitions under the brand name Ozeki.

The marvelous inlay work on Ozeki pieces is astonishing, but they seem over elaborate to Japanese tastes. On the other hand, this is an indication of Ozeki's success as a businessman, for he had a firm grasp of Western tastes. Ozeki remained in business throughout the Meiji period and into the subsequent Taisho era (1912–26).

Other companies did not simply commission works from artisans but actually established their own workshops. The most important of these were Komai and Jomi in Kyoto.

Though the Komai firm is believed to have been founded in 1841 by Komai Seibei, it was during the time of Komai Otojiro (1842–1917), regarded as the first-generation proprietor, that the workshop initially produced works displaying the renowned textured inlay in gold and silver.

At the age of thirteen, Komai Otojiro had the opportunity to study inlay techniques with Misaki Shusuke, a sword-fitting artisan from Higo. Otojiro produced sword fittings up until the 1876 prohibition against wearing swords, but in 1873 he had already begun to produce decorative objects aimed at the export market.

Komai Otojiro's delicate and highly detailed work was very well received abroad, and other artisans in Kyoto began to produce similar objects. The Komai firm continued to produce metalwork objects until 1941.

Jomi was equally successful in serving the export market. Jomi Eisuke studied metalworking under the ninth-generation Kanaya Gorosaburo and exhibited his works at many venues both in Japan and overseas. Jomi had two lines of work, medium and top quality, and had eighty-one workshops producing the medium-quality objects alone. The firm must have employed several hundred metalworkers.

So it was that at the start of the Meiji period numerous brokers and workshops were established and, with a clear understanding of the tastes of their Western customers, employed many artisans who had formerly produced sword fittings. Metalwork objects by Komai and Jomai still regularly appear on the auction blocks of London and New York. When a piece with the Ozeki brand comes up for sale, the bidding inevitably heats up and it sells easily for from ten to twenty million yen.

pp. 118–123

Lacquer

Lacquer objects with maki-e decorations were the first Japanese craft objects to be exported.

The Jesuit Francis Xavier arrived in Kagoshima in 1549 to bring Christianity to Japan, and the new religion spread quickly. Many of the Jesuit missionaries were delighted by the lacquerware they discovered here, with its gleaming gold designs and images, and they took to using lacquerware inlaid with mother-of-pearl ritual utensils, including reliquary boxes for portaits of the saints, ciborium (the box used to hold the communion wafers), and bible stands. The missionaries commissioned large numbers of ritual implements from Kyoto lacquer artisans making Kodaiji maki-e.

These implements attracted a great deal of interest back in Europe, and soon the Dutch East India Company—then present in Japan—was exporting lacquerware to Europe. They, too, placed orders directly with the lacquer artisans of Kyoto.

Kyoto was the center of maki-e lacquerware at the time. The most popular items among Europeans were chests, writing desks, and decorative coffers, and so-called Nanban ("Southern Barbarian," as Europeans were then known) lacquerware became an important Kyoto industry. Lacquerware from the period still frequently appears at auction in London and New York, and numerous lacquerware pieces from the Momoyama and Early Edo periods are to be found in European museums.

When the Tokugawa government closed the country, the export of Nanban lacquerware came to a sudden halt. The Japanese government decided to give exclusive (though very limited) trading rights to the Dutch and expelled all Spanish and Portuguese missionaries. Though Nanban wares were no longer produced and exported, lacquerware continued to be traded, and large quantities of lacquerware were exported from Japan through the settlement of Dejima off Nagasaki, where the Dutch were allowed to keep a small outpost.

Of the Japanese lacquerware exported to Europe during the Tokugawa or Edo period, the collection of small boxes prized by Queen of France Marie Antoinette (1755–93) is particularly famous. Now dispersed to Versailles, the Louvre, and the Guimet Museum, it is unclear whether the collection was actually assembled by Marie Antoinette or her mother, Empress Maria-Theresa of Austria, but it is certain that this collection of small boxes was exported from Japan by Dutch merchants on Dejima.

The beauty of Japanese lacquerware of the Momoyama and Edo periods was well known by the European aristocracy prior to the opening of Japan in 1868. When Japan participated for the first time in a world's fair, the Vienna World's Fair of 1873, the lacquerware it exhibited won the highest accolades, and from that moment on the best Japanese lacquerware suddenly began to be exported in great numbers.

At the same time, new styles of lacquerware, with shapes and designs consciously tailored to Western needs and tastes, began to be produced in the Meiji period in Tokyo and Yokohama. At first it was well received, but as poor-quality products with stultified and unoriginal designs flooded the market, it waned in popularity.

Concerned about this development, in 1891 lacquerware artisans formed the Japan Lacquer Association to restore the industry's high standards. When the Japanese government established the Tokyo Art School in 1889, it set up a lacquer department to insure the preservation and improvement of the craft. Leading Meiji-era lacquer artists and artists under the patronage of the imperial household such as Kawanobe Itcho (1830–1910), Ikeda Taishin, (1825–1903), and Shirayama Shosai (1853–1923) were charged with instructing successors to the craft, and they strove diligently to elevate the standards of their art.

Maki-e is one of many lacquerware techniques, and it is unique to Japan. The basic techniques were already perfected in the Heian period (794–1195), leading to the conclusion that they had existed in less refined forms from an earlier period.

Simply put, maki-e is the art of painting designs and images with the final coat of the lacquer, then sprinkling the images with gold and silver powders and placing the piece in a chamber with a controlled environment (called the *furo*) to dry. After drying the piece is polished with fine ash of various grades.

The actual process is actually quite complex and varied, and the *taka* maki-e (raised maki-e) and *togidashi* maki-e (burnished maki-e) techniques are especially time-consuming and demanding. Maki-e techniques continued to evolve over the centuries and reached their summit in the Late Edo and Meiji periods.

During the Edo period, maki-e flourished in Kyoto, Tokyo, and Kanazawa. When the imperial capital was transferred to Tokyo in the Meiji period and the government set about actively promoting export, the balance between the three production centers was upset. Tokyo was close to the port of Yokohama, and the majority of export lacquerware came to be produced in the Tokyo area. At the same time, much low-quality work was produced in Tokyo, and the area's reputation suffered, while Kanazawa and Kyoto continued to preserve traditional methods and produce high-quality lacquerware, though in a smaller volume.

Two decorative techniques frequently employed in lacquerware made for export in the Tokyo-Yokohama area are Shibayama décor and Somada décor. Both are new decorative techniques that emerged in the Late Edo period and were rarely employed in lacquerware intended for the domestic market.

Shibayama décor entailed the extensive use of inlay designs complemented by maki-e images. Ivory, shell, coral, tortoiseshell, and other materials are used for the inlay. The maki-e is applied to any remaining space. This design style was originated by Onogi Senzo of Sibayama, Shimosa Province (north-central Chiba Prefecture).

Somada décor employs thin strips of mother-of-pearl and gold leaf which are applied to the surface of the piece in intricate designs. It was originated by Somada Kiyosuke, a Kyoto craftsman who later worked in the Toyama fief.

The method of applying pieces of ivory, tortoiseshell, mother-of-pearl, and gold leaf to the surface of a piece had been used in lacquerware before the inception of the Shibayama and Somada styles, but maki-e had always been the main focus and other techniques played a secondary role. The newer styles reversed this relationship. They both enjoyed great popularity overseas and were produced in large quantities.

Both Shibayama and Somada-style pieces are very colorful and, at the same time, intricate and highly detailed. Traditional maki-e, on the other hand, were all gold or gold on a black lacquer background.

Shibayama pieces may have colorful red, orange, green, blue, and brown designs on a gold background. Somada pieces created beautiful images on the black lacquer surface by using the green, pink, and blue of mother-of-pearl and combining them with pieces of gold leaf.

It is easy to see why they were so popular in the West—indeed, one can't help but wonder why more weren't created for the Japanese market. The Meiji period was a time of many exciting new discoveries and vibrant trends in the art of maki-e.

pp. 136–141

Important Craft Objects of the Late Edo and Meiji Periods

Kazutoshi Harada
Special Research Chair
Tokyo National Museum

Japan has been influenced by Chinese and Korean arts and crafts from ancient times, but when were Japanese craft products first exported to and appreciated by people of other cultures? It seems clear that Japanese arts and crafts did not exert any stylistic influences on those of China and Korea, but were Japanese arts and crafts popular as items of trade?

In 1401, shogun Ashikaga Yoshimitsu sent the first trade mission to Ming-dynasty China, and in the subsequent trade with the Chinese, mainly conducted by the Ashikaga shoguns, maki-e and fans were the main craft objects exported from Japan. There is no direct evidence of how these items were received in China, but a record dated 1468 states that one hundred fans were sent to China in a black lacquer box decorated with a gold maki-e design of a dragon, and in 1451, 1,350 fans were exported. Naturally, fans were also being made in China at the time, so the fact that such a large number were shipped there must indicate that they had some feature or quality that the Chinese found attractive. The type of fan is not recorded, but they may well have resembled the fans presented in 1391 to Kumano Hayatama Shrine, with their depictions of trees and birds and flowers.

The craft objects treated in the present book are generally relatively small and characterized by elaborate designs and intricate production techniques. Perhaps no other nation has excelled at this kind of craft to the same extent as Japan. There are many small, high-quality Tang-dynasty silver pieces and Ming-dynasty snuff boxes delicately fashioned from materials such as ivory and jade, but the highly detailed craftsmanship that evolved across a wide range of crafts in Japan, particularly during the Edo period—metalwork, lacquerware, ceramics, and wood and ivory carvings—is unrivaled elsewhere. In Japan, these craft objects were implements of daily life. It was Europeans who first recognized them as works of art and began to collect them as such.

French queen Marie Antoinette (1755–93) is a well-known early collector of Japanese crafts. Her collection focused on small eighteenth-century lidded boxes in naturalistic shapes, such as gourds, dogs, and domestic fowl. It also included sets of five or six nested lacquerware boxes decorated with maki-e images; a jewel was often kept in the smallest, innermost box of the set. The first examples of maki-e to be exported to Europe are believed to have arrived there by Portuguese or Spanish ships at the end of the sixteenth century. Most of them were what used to be known in Japan as Nanban lacquer ("Nanban," meaning "southern barbarians," the common term for Europeans at the time). They were largely either Christian ritual implements or furnishings for the homes of the aristocracy, such as chests or coffers, and most were black lacquer with maki-e depictions of birds and flowers and extensive mother-of-pearl inlay decoration. The widespread appreciation of such objects in Europe at that time is evident from the many items preserved to this day in Europe's palaces and great homes. After Japan was closed to the outside world at the beginning of the Edo period, exports of some craft items continued through the Dutch settlement at Dejima.

Most of the crafts that became popular with Westerners after the country was opened again in 1868 had gone through a long evolution during the Edo period, beginning as purely functional objects and gradually growing increasingly refined in their construction and, in particular, their decoration. Sword fittings are a good example of this process. Prior to the Muromachi period, sword guards were mainly functional and made of unadorned iron. But as the short sword (*wakiszashi*) became a part of the costume of the samurai, to be worn at all times, sword fittings grew more decorative. A resident of the Nishijin district of Kyoto, Umetada Myoju, was one of the first to create intricate designs for sword guards using metals and alloys of different colors to produce inlay patterns and beautiful designs. The craft of decorated metalwork sword fittings later evolved into the metalwork objects that were exported in the Meiji period. Over the centuries, numerous techniques were developed, including various types of inlay—carved inlay, relief inlay, and overlay—engraving, and texturing through different types of chasing and chiseling. The metalwork objects that received such high accolades at world's fairs in the late nineteenth century can all be traced back to the craft of making decorative sword fittings.

The inro, netsuke, and ojime beads that enjoy such a high reputation today were also originally objects of every day use, part of an individual's wardrobe, and as such were produced in great quantities. Their mass production encouraged a constant evolution of technical and design innovations, and they have become the focus of collections around the world.

It was during the Meiji period that Japan's craft objects began to be collected extensively in the West, a trend encouraged by the display and sale of the objects at world's fairs. Starting with the Paris World's Fair in 1867, Japan participated in the 1873

Vienna World's Fair, the 1876 Philadelphia World's Fair, the 1878 Paris World's Fair, the 1889 Paris World's Fair, 1893 Chicago World's Fair, and the 1900 Paris World's Fair.

The response to the exhibitions and world fairs had a direct bearing on Japanese exports and foreign trade balance; as a result, the government made a concerted effort to research and appeal to Westerners' tastes. The efforts of such figures as art dealer Hayashi Tadamasa (1853–1906), pioneering graphic artist and arts educator Notomi Kaijiro (1844–1918), and painter Asai Chu (1856–1907) in this regard are well known.

Dr. Harris has also written of these exhibitions and fairs, but I would like to add a bit of information on the content of the displays. The products displayed at the 1867 Paris World's Fair were not manufactured specifically for the fair; instead, craft objects used in daily life in Japan were selected and exhibited without particular consideration of their value as commercial exports. But from the 1873 Vienna World's Fair, the craft products were manufactured specifically for the fair, with an eye to export value. In the category of metalwork, large, elaborately decorated, cast bronze vases and incense burners (that would have no use in Japan, but were popular as display objects in Victorian parlors) were exhibited, as well as smaller flower vases, dishes, and incense burners with highly detailed engraving and colorful applied overlay patterns of birds and flowers that Westerners found exotic and attractive. In the category of ceramics, intricately decorated and brightly colored Satsuma ware, Koransha, and Miyagawa Kozan productions were emphasized, as well as large ceramic garden lanterns and decorative plates from Arita and Seto. At the relatively early Vienna World's Fair, Late Edo lacquerware shelves and small chests, incense containers, and small boxes of the type that would have been used in Japan were exhibited, but from the Philadelphia World's Fair in 1876, Shibata Zeshin, Ikeda Taishin, Kawanobe Itcho, and other leading artists produced numerous lacquer paintings—a genre that was not at all popular among Japanese—depicting typically Japanese scenes. The production of lacquer paintings peaked at the 1893 Chicago World's Fair.

Participation in the first world fairs of the Meiji era was aimed at promoting Japanese exports, but by the Chicago World's Fair, one of the major goals of the Japanese was to have Japanese crafts and arts recognized as fine art suitable for museum display. This, it was felt, would be tantamount to the recognition of the Japanese nation and its culture as an equal to Western nations. There were both a crafts pavilion and an arts pavilion on the fair grounds. The art exhibits were categorized as sculpture, painting, and decorative arts (the latter subdivided into metalwork, ceramics, lacquerware, and so forth). The policy of the American sponsors was to display all pictorial arts, regardless of the medium, in the painting section of the arts pavilion, with the result that many Japanese craft works were displayed as paintings. For example, metalworkers Kano Natsuo and Unno Shomin made pictorial plaques using inlays of metals in various colors; ceramic artists created large vases with paintings of birds and flowers or Japanese scenes; lacquer artists likewise made plaques with pictorial depictions, such as Ikeda Taishin's depiction of Enoshima in lacquer. Even textile artists created pictorial works that were displayed with the paintings. Nishimura Jihei's birds-and-flowers folding screen, Tanaka Rihichi's folding screen depicting peacocks, and Kawashima Jinbei's birds-and-flowers wall hanging, though all textiles, were displayed as paintings.

At the Chicago World's Fair, metalworker Suzuki Chokichi's *Twelve Hawks* (fig. 1) earned special praise. A work of stunning visual impact with its many-colored metal inlays, it was praised not only in Chicago but in newspapers throughout the United States. In response to this positive reception, the Japanese world's fair office issued a statement providing further information on the nature of Japanese crafts, emphasizing their intricate detailing and highly refined color sensibility.

Interestingly, the inro, netsuke, and sword fittings so popular today with Westerners were not exhibited at the world fairs. Perhaps this was because they were already recognized as valuable private collector's objects. During the *Japonisme* movement that began in the 1850s, Westerners were already purchasing these objects in Japan and sending them home, where they were being carefully catalogued and studied. In 1881, Edmond de Goncourt (of the famous Goncourt publishing dynasty) wrote a study of netsuke, and in 1883 Louis Gonse published a book on sword guards. From 1881 to 1891, S. Bingga published a journal on Japanese art titled *Le Japon Artistique*.

From about this time the first major collectors of Japanese craft objects appeared, among them the French Mrs. Clémence d'Ennery (wife of the famous dramatic author Adolphe d'Ennery), Émile Étienne Guimet, and Henri Cernuschi; the Italians Edoardo Chiossone and Pierre Garda; and the early twentieth-century Swiss Alfred Baur. Chiossone was a sculptor who worked for the Paper Currency Bureau (now the Printing Bureau, Ministry of Finance), and he died in Japan, which means that his entire collection was assembled there. The others purchased their collections in Europe or through Japanese dealers. The d'Ennery collection is located in a private home near the Guimet Museum. The second floor is an exhibition space, and at the top of the stairs the visitor is treated to an art nouveau wood case completely filled with lions, from Ming and Ching celadons, yellow and red-glazed wares, to colorful Imari figures. Other cases around the room contain human and animal figures categorized by type or theme. There are maki-e incense containers decorated with tiny, finely wrought depictions of animals, people, musical instruments, furniture, and fruits. The netsuke are interestingly displayed in a case about 60 centimeters on a side, rising up in a pyramid. The atmosphere is quite unlike anything contemporary museum viewers might expect (fig. 2). The pieces are displayed just as they were by the owners, who in fact used to live in the house with their collection. Mrs. d'Ennery donated the collection to the French nation on her death, but on the condition that neither the cases nor their contents be moved or rearranged. In other words, when one visits the collection one can experience exactly the tastes and pleasures of its owner one hundred years ago. The visitor can partake of her view of Japanese crafts.

The Western appreciation of Japanese prints is well known, and the same was true of such Late Edo and Meiji period crafts as inro, netsuke, and sword fittings. Europeans were the first to value these objects highly. The fact that they are small and easy to transport may have contributed to this. There are many Meiji-period craft objects that were produced specifically for export—for example, Shibayama lacquerware, with its highly decorative designs combining maki-e, mother-of-pearl, ivory, and precious metals. In metalwork, there are cast bronzes from the Miyao workshop, inlaid with gold and silver, depicting samurai, sumo wrestlers, and townspeople; Komai-workshop metalwork productions, large dishes, pagodas, or chests made of iron and completely covered with intricate arabesque or other patterns in a texture of gold and silver inlay; and Takase Kozan works, usually animal figures such as lobsters or insects made of iron, copper, and silver with fully articulated, moveable limbs. In addition, an enormous number of other craft objects, including the wired cloisonné of Namikawa Yasuyuki in Kyoto, were produced. Such craft objects are frequently seen not only in Western museums but also galleries and auction houses, but they are very rare in Japan. Most of the research on them is also by necessity carried out by Western scholars and collectors.

Today an increasing number of art lovers like the author of this work, Masayuki Murata, are making an effort to purchase the craft masterpieces of the Late Edo and Meiji periods and repatriate them. To date most research on the crafts of that period have focused on the works of the leading artisans, but it is important to study the objects made for export to gain a complete picture of the wonderful crafts of Late Edo and Meiji.

Editorial note: All of the objects featured in the present work are from the collection of the Kiyomizu Sannenzaka Museum. The brief essays on Late Edo and Meiji-period crafts by Masayuki MURATA originally appeared ins lightly different form as a series in the *Kyoto Shimbun* from July 2005 through April 2005. In the case of netsuke and inro, "signed" indicates the craftman's art name. In some cases the workshop is noted. Except for the essay by Victor Harris, the English text has been translated from the Japanese with some adaptations to accommodate English readers.

収録作品一覧
List of Objects

1 桜蝶図平皿
［さくらちょうずひらざら］
並河靖之作　1845-1927
Plate with butterflies and cherry blossoms
NAMIKAWA Yasuyuki

2 蝶図瓢形花瓶
［ちょうずひさごがたかびん］
並河靖之作　1845-1927
Gourd-shaped vase with butterflies
NAMIKAWA Yasuyuki

3 花蝶文花瓶
［かちょうもんかびん］
並河靖之作　1845-1927
Vase with design of flowers and butterflies
NAMIKAWA Yasuyuki

4 藤図花瓶
［ふじずかびん］
並河靖之作　1845-1927
Vase with wisteria
NAMIKAWA Yasuyuki

5-6 春秋遊技図扁壺　一対
［しゅんじゅうゆうぎずへんこ　いっつい］
並河靖之作　1845-1927
Pair of drum vases depicting spring and autumn pastimes
NAMIKAWA Yasuyuki

7 花鳥図花瓶
［かちょうずかびん］
並河靖之作　1845-1927
Vase with birds and flowers
NAMIKAWA Yasuyuki

8 蝶草花文飾り壺
［ちょうそうかもんかざりつぼ］
並河靖之作　1845-1927
Jar with design of flowers and butterflies
NAMIKAWA Yasuyuki

9 花蝶文飾り壺
［かちょうもんかざりつぼ］
並河靖之作　1845-1927
Jar with design of flowers and butterflies
NAMIKAWA Yasuyuki

10 花文飾り壺
［はなもんかざりつぼ］
並河靖之作　1845-1927
Jar with floral design
NAMIKAWA Yasuyuki

11 蝶図香合
［ちょうずこうごう］
並河靖之作　1845-1927
Incense container with butterflies
NAMIKAWA Yasuyuki

12 花鳥図棗
［かちょうずなつめ］
並河靖之作　1845-1927
Tea container with birds and flowers
NAMIKAWA Yasuyuki

13 花蝶文香水瓶
［かちょうもんこうすいびん］
並河靖之作　1845-1927
Perfume bottles with design of butterflies and flowers
NAMIKAWA Yasuyuki

14 花文飾り壺
［はなもんかざりつぼ］
並河靖之作　1845-1927
Jars with floral design
NAMIKAWA Yasuyuki

15 花鳥図飾り壺
［かちょうずかざりつぼ］
並河靖之作　1845-1927
Jar with birds and flowers
NAMIKAWA Yasuyuki

16 芦カワセミ図飾り壺
［あしかわせみずかざりつぼ］
並河靖之作　1845-1927
Jar with kingfisher and reeds
NAMIKAWA Yasuyuki

17 紅葉鳥図飾り壺
［もみじとりずかざりつぼ］
並河靖之作　1845-1927
Jar with birds and autumn foliage
NAMIKAWA Yasuyuki

18 山水図香炉
［さんすいずこうろ］
並河靖之作　1845-1927
Incense burner with landscape
NAMIKAWA Yasuyuki

19 葵祭図花瓶　一対
［あおいまつりずかびん　いっつい］
並河靖之作　1845-1927
Pair of vases with festival scene
NAMIKAWA Yasuyuki

20 四季草花図花瓶
［しきそうかずかびん］
林小伝治作　1831-1915
Vase with flowers of the four seasons
HAYASHI Kodenji

21 花鳩図花瓶
[はなはとずかびん]
林小伝治作　1831-1915
Vase with doves and flowers
HAYASHI Kodenji

22 蝶図花瓶
[ちょうずかびん]
林小伝治作　1831-1915
Vase with butterflies
HAYASHI Kodenji

23 鳥図香合
[とりずこうごう]
林小伝治作　1831-1915
Incense container with birds
HAYASHI Kodenji

24 蝶図小箱
[ちょうずこばこ]
林小伝治作　1831-1915
Small box with butterflies
HAYASHI Kodenji

25-26 藤図飾り壺
[ふじずかざりつぼ]
林小伝治作　1831-1915
Jar with wisteria
HAYASHI Kodenji

27 花鳥図花瓶
[かちょうずかびん]
林小伝治作　1831-1915
Vase with birds and flowers
HAYASHI Kodenji

28-29 群蝶文小箱
[ぐんちょうもんこばこ]
粂野締太郎作　1863-1939
Small box with pattern of flocking butterflies
KUMENO Teitaro

30-31 粟鶉図鉢
[あわうずらずはち]
川出柴太郎作　1856-?
Squared flower-petal bowl with quail and millet
KAWADE Shibataro

32 深山雉図花瓶
[しんざんきじずかびん]
伊藤銘
Vase with pheasants and mountain scene
Signed "ITO"

33 牡丹図花瓶
[ぼたんずかびん]
服部唯三郎作
Vase with peonies
HATTORI Tadasaburo

34 龍鳳凰文花瓶
[りゅうほうおうもんかびん]
安藤重兵衛作
Vase with dragon and phoenix design
ANDO Jubei

35 紅葉草花図花瓶
[もみじそうかずかびん]
無銘
Vase with autumn foliage and flowers
No signature

36 鷹図花瓶
[たかずかびん]
無銘
Vase with hawk
No signature

37 牡丹図花瓶
[ぼたんずかびん]
無銘
Vase with peonies
No signature

38 舟鷺図皿
[ふねさぎずさら]
涛川惣助作　1847-1910
Decorative plate boat with and heron
NAMIKAWA Sosuke

39-40 糸桜図皿
[いとざくらずさら]
惣助銘「魁」
涛川惣助作　1847-1910
Decorative plate with weeping cherry
NAMIKAWA Sosuke

41 藤図花瓶
[ふじずかびん]
涛川惣助作　1847-1910
Vase with wisteria
NAMIKAWA Sosuke

42 紅白芙蓉図小箱
[こうはくふようずこばこ]
涛川惣助作　1847-1910
Small box with white and red mallow flowers
NAMIKAWA Sosuke

43 富嶽図煙草ケース
[ふがくずたばこけーす]
涛川惣助作　1847-1910
Cigarette case with view of Mount Fuji
NAMIKAWA Sosuke

44 富嶽図小箱
[ふがくずこばこ]
涛川惣助作　1847-1910
Small box with view of Mount Fuji
NAMIKAWA Sosuke

45 菊紋月芦雁図花瓶 一対
［きくもんつきあしかりずかびん　いっつい］

涛川惣助作　1847-1910
Pair of vases with wild goose and reeds
and chrysanthemum crests
NAMIKAWA Sosuke

46-47 菊紋蛍図花瓶 一対
［きくもんほたるずかびん　いっつい］

涛川惣助作　1847-1910
Pair of vases with fireflies and chrysanthemum crests
NAMIKAWA Sosuke

48 色絵金彩組輪文茶碗（部分拡大）
［いろえきんさいくみわもんちゃわん］

司山製
Tea bowl with design of concentric circles
on colors and gold
SHIZAN workshop

49 色絵金彩花鳥図花瓶
［いろえきんさいかちょうずかびん］

7代目錦光山宗兵衛製　1868-1927
Vase with birds and flowers in colors and gold
KINKOZAN Sobei VII workshop

50 色絵金彩花見図花瓶
［いろえきんさいはなみずかびん］

7代目錦光山宗兵衛製　1868-1927
Vase with cherry-blossom viewing scene
in colors and gold
KINKOZAN Sobei VII workshop

51 色絵金彩花鳥図花瓶
［いろえきんさいかちょうずかびん］

7代目錦光山宗兵衛製　1868-1927
Vase with birds and flowers in colors and gold
KINKOZAN Sobei VII workshop

52-53 色絵金彩花鶏図茶碗
［いろえきんさいかけいずちゃわん］

版錦山製
Tea bowl with flowers and domestic fowl in colors and gold
HANKINZAN workshop

54 色絵金彩花蝶文鉢
［いろえきんさいかちょうもんはち］

作者不詳
Bowl with design of birds and butterflies
in colors and gold
Artist unknown

55 色絵金彩洋花図鉢
［いろえきんさいようばなずはち］

7代目錦光山宗兵衛製
Bowl with Western flowers in colors and gold
KINKOZAN Sobei VII workshop

56 色絵金彩菊図輪花鉢
［いろえきんさいきくずりんかばち］

源山
Scalloped bowl with chrysanthemums in colors and gold
GENZAN

57-58 色絵金彩浦島太郎図貝合せ
［いろえきんさいうらしまたろうずかいあわせ］

陽山製
Decorative clam shells with scenes from the folk tale
Urashima Taro in colors and gold
YOZAN workshop

59 色絵金彩扇面文飾り壺
［いろえきんさいせんめんもんかざりつぼ］

古山製
Jar with design of folding fans in colors and gold
KOZAN workshop

60 色絵金彩祭礼図飾り壺
［いろえきんさいさいれいずかざりつぼ］

司山製
Jar with festival scene in colors and gold
SHIZAN workshop

61-62 色絵金彩蝶菊尽し茶碗
［いろえきんさいちょうきくづくしちゃわん］

藪　明山製　1853-1934
Tea bowl with banded pattern of butterflies
and chrysanthemums
YABU Meizan workshop

63 色絵金彩鶴花人物図花瓶 一対
［いろえきんさいつるはなじんぶつずかびん　いっつい］

藪　明山製　1853-1934
Pair of vases with cranes, flowers, and human figures
YABU Meizan workshop

64-65 夕立雨宿り蒔絵印籠
［ゆうだちあまやどりまきえいんろう］

塩見政誠銘
Inro with maki-e depiction of taking
shelter from a sudden evening shower
Signed "SHIOMI Masanari"

66-67 蘭陵王蒔絵印籠
［らんりょうおうまきえいんろう］

梶川文龍斎銘
金工：浜野矩随作
Inro with maki-e depiction of a Bugaku court dance
Signed "KAJIKAWA Bunryusai"
Metalwork: HAMANO Noriyuki

68 伊勢海老蒔絵印籠（シャンプーコレクション）
［いせえびまきえいんろう］

自徳銘
Inro with maki-e depiction of lobsters
Signed "JITOKU"

69 猫蝶牡丹蒔絵印籠（シャンプーコレクション）
[ねこちょうぼたんまきえいんろう]

寿秀銘
Inro with maki-e depiction of a cat, butterflies, and peony
Signed "TOSHIHIDE"

70-71 群盲撫象蒔絵印籠
[ぐんもうぶぞうまきえいんろう]

梶川銘
Inro with maki-e depiction of the parable of the blind men examining an elephant
Signed "KAJIKAWA"

72-73 節句蒔絵印籠（シャンプーコレクション）
[せっくまきえいんろう]

春照斎銘
Inro with maki-e depiction of seasonal festivals
Signed "SHUNSHOSAI"

74-75 祇園祭礼蒔絵印籠
[ぎおんさいれいまきえいんろう]

春正銘
Inro with maki-e depiction of the Gion Festival
Signed "SHUNSHO"

76-77 合戦蒔絵印籠
[かっせんまきえいんろう]

無銘
Inro with maki-e depiction of battle scene
No signature

78-79 群鶴蒔絵印籠
[ぐんかくまきえいんろう]

無銘
Inro with maki-e depiction of flock of cranes
No signature

80 千羽鶴蒔絵印籠
[せんばづるまきえいんろう]

常川銘
Inro with maki-e depiction of thousand crane-pattern
Signed "JOSEN"

81 群蝶蒔絵青貝印籠
[ぐんちょうまきえあおがいいんろう]

観松斎銘
Inro with maki-e and mother-of-pearl depiction of butterflies
Signed "KANSHOSAI"

82-83 絵馬蒔絵印籠
[えままきえいんろう]

幸阿弥銘
Inro with maki-e depiction of Shinto talismans featuring horse and monkey figures
Signed "KOAMI"

84-85 吉原蒔絵印籠
[よしわらまきえいんろう]

松杖斎銘
Inro with maki-e depiction of the Yoshiwara pleasure quarters
Signed "SHOJOSAI"

86 歌舞伎寿曽我対面蒔絵印籠
（シャンプーコレクション）
[かぶきことぶきそがのたいめんまきえいんろう]

春政銘
Inro with maki-e depiction of scene from a Kabuki play
Signed "HARUMASA"

87-88 傘美人蒔絵印籠
[かさびじんまきえいんろう]

春正銘
Inro with maki-e depiction of beauties under a parasol and a youthful dandy
Signed "SHUNSHO"

89-90 川中島合戦金工鞘印籠
[かわなかじまかっせんきんこうさやいんろう]

一柳友善銘
Sheath inro with metal-inlay depiction of the Battle of Kawanakajima
Signed "ICHIRYU Tomoyoshi"

91 平田七宝印籠
[ひらたしっぽういんろう]

無銘
Inro with Hirata cloisonné
No signature

92-93 獅子牡丹金工印籠
[ししぼたんきんこういんろう]

大川元義・小泉友随合作
緒締め：義茂銘
Inro with metal inlay depiction of lion and peony
OKAWA Motoyoshi and KOIZUMI Tomoyuki
Ojime: signed "YOSHISHIGE"

94 恵比寿大黒杣田印籠
[えびすだいこくそまだいんろう]

杣田久光銘
Somada-lacquer inro depicting the gods Ebisu and Daikoku
Signed "SOMADA Hisamitsu"

95 菊花堆朱印籠
[きっかついしゅいんろう]

無銘
Inro with chrysanthemum pattern in carved red lacquer (*tsuishu*)
No signature

96-97 杯蠅木彫・金工根付
[さかづきはえもくちょう・きんこうねつけ]

天民銘
Netsuke of fly in a bowl, wood and metal
Signed "TENMIN"

98 束ね薪蒔絵印籠
[たばねたきぎまきえいんろう]

観松斎銘

紅葉蒔絵瓢形根付・堆朱瓢形緒締
[もみじまきえひさごがたねつけ・ついしゅひさごがたおじめ]

Inro in the shape of firewood and gourd with maki-e decoration
Signed "KANSHOSAI"
Gourd-shaped netsuke with maki-e of fall foliage, carved red lacquer gourd-shaped ojime

99 秋草蒔絵鞘印籠
[あきくさまきえさやいんろう]

観松斎銘

蕨図金工根付（加納夏雄作）・珊瑚緒締め
[わらびずきんこうねつけ・さんごおじめ]

Sheath inro with maki-e depiction of autumn grasses
Signed "KANSHOSAI"
Metalwork netsuke in fern frond design (KANO Natsuo), coral ojime

100 猿回し金工鏡蓋根付
[さるまわしきんこうかがみぶたねつけ]

なつを銘（加納夏雄作）

Kagamibuta netsuke with metal inlay design of a monkey trainer and monkey
Signed "NATSUO" (KANO Natsuo)

101 草花象牙彫饅頭根付
[そうかぞうげぼりまんじゅうねつけ]

無銘

Ivory *manju* netsuke with carved floral design
No signature

102-103 花虫金工鏡蓋根付
[はなむしきんこうかがみぶたねつけ]

無銘

Kagamibuta netsuke with metal inlay design of flowers and insects
No signature

104 銀杏象牙彫根付
[ぎんなんぞうげぼりねつけ]

光春銘

Ivory netsuke carved in the shape of gingko nuts
Signed "KOSHUN"

105-106 蛸象牙彫根付
[たこぞうげぼりねつけ]

正水

Ivory netsuke carved in the shape of an octopus
Signed "SHOSUI"

107-108 親子亀象牙彫根付
[おやこがめぞうげぼりねつけ]

無銘

Ivory netsuke carved in the shape of parent and child turtles
No signature

109 蜂巣木彫・象牙彫根付
[はちすもくちょう・ぞうげぼりねつけ]

忠一銘

Wood netsuke carved in the shape of hornet's nest with ivory insets as larvae
Signed "TADAICHI"

110-111 梨蜂木彫根付
[なしはちもくちょうねつけ]

江月銘

Wood netsuke carved in the shape of wasp and pear
Signed "KOGETSU"

112-113 蟬木彫根付
[せみもくちょうねつけ]

無銘

Wood netsuke carved in the shape of cicada
No signature

114 落花生木彫根付
[らっかせいもくちょうねつけ]

玉藻銘

Wood netsuke carved in the shape of peanuts
Signed "GYOKUSO"

115 栗木彫根付
[くりもくちょうねつけ]

藻水銘

Wood netsuke carved in the shape of chestnut
Signed "SOSUI"

116 蛇籠木彫根付
[じゃかごもくちょうねつけ]

旭舟銘

Wood netsuke carved in the shape of gravel-filled basket used to reinforce river banks
Signed "KYOKUSHU"

117 銭束木彫根付
[ぜにたばもくちょうねつけ]

旭斎銘

Wood netsuke carved in the shape of string of coins
Signed "KYUSAI"

118 蛇木彫根付
[へびもくちょうねつけ]

無銘

Wood netsuke carved in the shape of snake
No signature

119-120 越後獅子木彫根付
[えちごじしもくちょうねつけ]

珉江銘

Wood netsuke carved in the shape of Echigo-*jishi* (mythical lion)
Signed "MINKO"

121-122 獅子木彫根付
[ししもくちょうねつけ]

無銘

Wood netsuke carved in the shape of *shishi* (mythical lion)
No signature

123 人魚木彫根付
［にんじょもくちょうねつけ］
一雲銘
Wood netsuke carved in the shape of mermaid
Signed "ICHIUN"

124 烏天狗木彫根付
［からすてんぐもくちょうねつけ］
舟珉銘
Wood netsuke carved in the shape of *tengu* goblin
Signed "SHUMIN"

125-127 蝶紋金総金具堆黒鞘合口拵え
［ちょうもんきんそうかなぐついこくさやあいくちこしらえ］
正阿弥勝義作　1832-1908
Carved black lacquer scabbard with gold fittings
SHOAMI Katsuyoshi

128-131 鶴亀図大小鐔
［つるかめずだいしょうつば］
佐野直好作　江戸中－後期
Small and large sword guards with crane and tortoise design
SANO Naoyoshi

132 猛禽狙猿図縁頭
［もうきんそえんずふちがしら］
大森英秀作　江戸後期
Sword collar depicting bird of prey stalking a monkey
OMORI Teruhide

133 牡丹図三所物
［ぼたんずみところもの］
後藤光保作　江戸後期
Sword accessories (hair pick, knife handle, hilt ornament) with peony pattern
GOTO Mitsuyasu

134-135 草花小禽図鐔
［そうかしょうきんずつば］
後藤一乗作　1791-1876
Sword guard with bird-and-flower design
GOTO Ichijo

136-137 茶釜図鐔
［ちゃがまずつば］
田中清寿作　1804-1876
Sword guard with tea kettle design
TANAKA Kiyotoshi

138-139 四季花鳥図大小鐔
［しきかちょうずだいしょうつば］
石黒是常作　江戸後期
Small and large sword guards with birds and flowers of the four seasons
ISHIGURO Koretsune

140-141 群鶏図二所物
［ぐんけいずふたところもの］
石黒英明作　江戸後期－明治初期
Knife handle and hair pick with design of domestic fowl
ISHIGURO Hideaki

142-143 鳳凰瑞雲図鐔
［ほうおうずいうんずつば］
三宅英光（自立軒）作　江戸後期
Sword guards with phoenix and clouds design
MIYAKE Terumitsu (JIRYUKEN)

144 蓬莱山図小柄
［ほうらいさんずこづか］
橋本一至作　1820-1896
Knife handle with depiction of Mount Horai
HASHIMOTO Isshi

145 粟穂図目貫
［あわほずめぬき］
荒木東明作　1817-1870
Hilt ornament with millet spray design
ARAKI Tomei

146 かちかち山図目貫
［かちかちやまずめぬき］
天光堂秀国作　1825-1891
Hilt Ornament depicting the *Kachikachiyama* folk tale
TENKODO Hidekuni

147-148 牡丹図鐔
［ぼたんずつば］
中村一行常親作　江戸後期
Sword guard with design of peonies
NAKAMURA Ikko Tsunechika

149-150 吉野川図鐔
［よしのがわずつば］
中村有宣作　江戸後期
Sword guard with design of Yoshino River
NAKAMURA Arinobu

151-152 月雁図鐔
［つきかりずつば］
青龍斎秀寿作　江戸後期
Sword guard with design of wild goose and the moon
SEIRYUSAI Hidetoshi

153-154 鳳凰図七宝鐔
［ほうおうずしっぽうつば］
平田玄斎作　江戸後期－明治初期
Sword guard with cloisonné of phoenix
HIRATA Gensai

155 胡蝶舞図小柄
［こちょうまいずこづか］
端信盧作　1803-?
Knife handle with design depicting ancient court dance *Kochomai*
HATA Nobuyoshi

156 萩流水図縁頭
[はぎりゅうすいずふちがしら]

荒井辰成作　江戸後期

Sword collar with design of bush clover
and a rushing stream
ARAI Tatsunari

157-161 四季花鳥図揃金具
[しきかちょうずそろいかなぐ]

鈴木美彦作　1884-1969

鐔－風吹牡丹図
目貫－春秋花鳥図
小柄－雪中鷺図

Complete set of sword accessories decorated with
birds and flowers of the four seasons
SUZUKI Yoshihiko
Sword guard with windblown peonies design
Hilt decoration depicting spring and
autumn birds (bush warbler and quail)
Knife handle with design of heron in the snow

162-163 蓮図鐔
[はすずつば]

加納夏雄作　1828-1898

Sword guard with lotus design
KANO Natsuo

164-165 アイリス図鐔
[あいりすずつば]

加納夏雄作　1828-1898

Sword guard with iris design
KANO Natsuo

166-167 群鶏図香炉
[ぐんけいずこうろ]

正阿弥勝義作　1832-1908

Incense burner with domestic fowls
SHOAMI Katsuyoshi

168 龍虎図花瓶 一対
[りゅうこずかびん　いっつい]

海野勝珉作　1844-1915

Pair of vases with tiger and dragon
UNNO Shomin

169 雀かたばみ図煙草ケース
[すずめかたばみずたばこけーす]

海野勝珉作　1844-1915

Cigarette case with sparrows and wood sorrel
UNNO Shomin

170 孔雀図宝石箱
[くじゃくずほうせきばこ]

飴谷有眠作　?-1939

Jewelry box with peacock
AMETANI Yumin

171 紅葉桜図香合
[もみじさくらずこうごう]

正阿弥勝義作　1832-1908

Incense container with maple leaves and cherry blossoms
SHOAMI Katsuyoshi

172 芍薬図懐中時計蓋
[しゃくやくずかいちゅうどけいふた]

加納夏雄作　1828-1898

Watchcase with peony
KANO Natsuo

173 押合菊香合
[おしあいぎくこうごう]

大森雪峰英友作　江戸後期

Incense container with relief chrysanthemums
OMORI Seppo Hidetomo

174 鷺図花瓶 一対
[さぎずかびん　いっつい]

香川勝広作　1853-1917

Pair of vases with herons
KAGAWA Katsuhiro

175 牡丹雀図一輪挿し
[ぼたんすずめずいちりんざし]

小林親光作　明治－大正期

Bud vase with peony and sparrow
KOBAYASHI Chikamitsu

176 菊図花瓶
[きくずかびん]

高玉斎一久作　江戸後期

Vase with chrysanthemums
KOGYOKUSAI Ikkyu

177 桜雉図花瓶
[さくらきじずかびん]

佐藤秀広作　1846-1925

Vase with cherry blossoms and pheasants
SATO Hidehiro

178 市井図香炉
[しせいずこうろ]

海野盛寿（凌雲斎）作　1834-1896

Incense burner with well-side scene
UNNO Moritoshi (RYOUNSAI)

179 草花図金象嵌銀製香炉
[そうかずきんぞうがんぎんせいこうろ]

無銘

Silver incense burner with overlay gold areas
in floral design
No signature

180 古代文唐草象嵌香炉
[こだいもんからくさぞうがんこうろ]

無銘

Incense burner with inlaid ancient-style
Chinese arabesque pattern
No signature

181 草花文布目象嵌香炉
[そうかもんぬのめぞうがんこうろ]

駒井製

Incense burner with inlaid floral designs
in textured panels
KOMAI workshop

182 花鳥図鉄地布目象嵌香炉
[かちょうずてつじぬのめぞうがんこうろ]
鹿島一谷作　1846-1925
Iron incense burner with textured panels depicting birds and flowers
KAJIMA Ikkoku

183-184 十香図蒔絵文庫
[じゅっこうずまきえぶんこ]
川之辺一朝作　1830-1910
Letter box with maki-e design of fragrant flowers
KAWANOBE Itcho

185-186 散り紅葉図蒔絵板文庫
[ちりもみじずまきえいたぶんこ]
池田泰真作　1825-1903
Wood letter box with pattern of falling autumn foliage in maki-e relief
IKEDA Taishin

187 籬秋草蒔絵木瓜形小箱
[まがきあきくさまきえきうりがたこばこ]
芝舩作
Small box with maki-e design of bamboo fence and autumn plants
Signed "SHISEN"

188 猫孔雀羽根図蒔絵入れ子小箱
[ねこくじゃくはねずまきえいれここばこ]
無銘
Inset box set, outer box with maki-e depiction of cat playing with peacock feathers,
two inner boxes decorated with fighting cocks
No signature

189-190 花尽くし図蒔絵重小箱
[はなづくしずまきえじゅうこばこ]
飯塚桃葉作　江戸後期
Set of stacking boxes with maki-e floral designs
IIZUKA Toyo

191 撫子図蒔絵小箱
[なでしこずまきえこばこ]
無銘
Small box with maki-e wild carnations
No signature

192-193 宇治川先陣図蒔絵小箱
[うじがわせんじんずまきえこばこ]
沢田宗沢斎作　1830-1915
Small box with maki-e depiction of the attack on Uji River
SAWADA Sotakusai

194 渦文蒔絵香合
[うずもんまきえこうごう]
白山松哉作　1853-1923
Incense container with ripple pattern
SHIRAYAMA Shosai

195 菊文蒔絵棗
[きくもんまきえなつめ]
白山松哉作　1853-1923
Tea container with maki-e chrysanthemum pattern
SHIRAYAMA Shosai

196 菊文蒔絵香合
[きくもんまきえこうごう]
白山松哉作　1853-1923
Incense container with maki-e chrysanthemum pattern
SHIRAYAMA Shosai

197-198 日月烏鷺図蒔絵額 一対
[じつげつうろずまきえがく　いっつい]
白山松哉作　1853-1923
Pair of lacquer plaques, sun and herons (left), moon and crow (right)
SHIRAYAMA Shosai

199-200 花尽くし図蒔絵香箱
[はなづくしずまきえこうばこ]
無銘
Incense box with maki-e floral design
No signature

201-202 乗合船図蒔絵硯箱
[のりあいぶねずまきえすずりばこ]
無銘
Writing box with maki-e depiction of a ferry boat
No signature

203 桜樹下鶏図小箱
[さくらじゅかとりずこばこ]
杣田細工
Small box with cock beneath a cherry tree
SOMADA style

204-205 狐の嫁入り図入れ子小箱
[きつねのよめいりずいれここばこ]
杣田細工
Inset box set with depiction of foxes' wedding
SOMADA style

206-207 花雉図蒔絵小箱
[はなきじずまきえこばこ]
芝山細工
Small box with maki-e depiction of flowers and pheasant
SHIBAYAMA style

208-209 四季草花図蒔絵提箪笥
[しきそうかずまきえさげだんす]
赤塚自得作　1871-1936
Portable chest with maki-e depiction of flowers of the four seasons
AKATSUKA Jitoku

The Author

Masayuki MURATA was born in 1950 in Kyoto. He is the owner and director of the Kiyomizu Sannenzaka Museum, which he established in September 2000, and the director of the Namikawa Yasuyuki Cloisonné Foundation. Mr. Murata has a strong interest in and appreciation for Late Edo and Meiji-period crafts and has long focused on collecting cloisonné metalwork, sword fittings, inro, and maki-e overseas and returning them to Japan. The Kiyomizu Sannenzaka Museum boasts one of the finest international collections of such objects both in terms of breadth and quality. Mr. Murata is also engaged in various efforts to research and revive the high level of craftsmanship reached in the Meiji period.

Kiyomizu Sannenzaka Museum

337-1 Kiyomizu-sanchome, Sanneizaka-kita-iru,
Kiyomizudera-monzen, Higashiyama-ku,
Kyoto 605-0862
Tel. 075-532-4270 Fax. 075-532-4271
Website: http://www.sannenzaka-museum.co.jp/

English translation: Jeffrey Hunter

Translation of
Victor Harris article into Japanese: Tetsuo KINOSHITA

Book design: UNO Yasuyuki Design Studio

Photography: Yoichi KIMURA, Sumiharu TAWARA

The publisher wishes to acknowledge the cooperation of Ribun Shuppan Co., Ltd.; and Hase Homando.

著者プロフィール

村田理如 むらた まさゆき

1950年、京都に生まれる。清水三年坂美術館館長、並河靖之有線七宝記念財団理事。
幕末・明治期を中心とする日本の細密工芸を高く評価し、その収集と紹介に尽力し、2000年9月、京都・東山区に清水三年坂美術館を開設。とりわけ七宝・金工・刀装具・印籠・蒔絵作品などには早い時期から注目し、海外へ流出した優品の買い戻しにつとめ、同館は幕末・明治期の細密工芸分野では質量ともに世界屈指の収蔵をほこる。また明治期に作られたハイレベルな作品やその技術の復元をめざし、研究機関を設置するなど、積極的な活動を展開している。

清水三年坂美術館
〒605-0862
京都市東山区清水寺門前三寧坂北入清水3丁目337-1
Tel. 075-532-4270 Fax. 075-532-4271
http://www.sannenzaka-museum.co.jp/

和文英訳：ジェフリー ハンター

英文和訳：木下哲夫

ブック・デザイン：宇野泰行デザイン室

撮影：木村羊一
　　No. 1-38, 41, 46-49, 51-67, 70, 71, 74-85, 87-95, 98, 99, 128-137, 142-161, 168-202, 206-209

　　俵　純治
　　No. 39, 40, 42-45, 50, 68, 69, 72, 73, 86, 96, 97, 100-127, 138-141, 162-167, 203-205

協力：(株) 里文出版
　　長谷宝満堂

世界を魅了した日本の技と美
幕末・明治の工芸

2006年2月14日　　初版発行
2015年8月 8日　　五版発行

著　者　　村田理如
発行人　　納屋嘉人
発行所　　株式会社　淡交社
本　社　　〒603-8588　京都市北区堀川通鞍馬口上ル
　　　　　営業　075-432-5151
　　　　　編集　075-432-5161
支　社　　〒162-0061　東京都新宿区市谷柳町 39-1
　　　　　営業　03-5269-7941
　　　　　編集　03-5269-1691
　　　　　http://www.tankosha.co.jp

印刷・製本　　大日本印刷株式会社

© 2006 MURATA Masayuki
Printed in Japan
ISBN978-4-473-03299-7

落丁・乱丁本がございましたら、小社「出版営業部」宛にお送りください。
送料小社負担にてお取り替えいたします。
本書の無断複写は、著作権法上での例外を除き、禁じられています。